The Seed

Finding Purpose and Happiness in Life and Work

JON GORDON

John Wiley & Sons, Inc.

Copyright © 2011 by Jon Gordon. All rights reserved.

Published by John Wiley & Sons, Inc., Hoboken, New Jersey.
Published simultaneously in Canada.

No part of this publication may be reproduced, stored in a retrieval system, or transmitted in any form or by any means, electronic, mechanical, photocopying, recording, scanning, or otherwise, except as permitted under Section 107 or 108 of the 1976 United States Copyright Act, without either the prior written permission of the Publisher, or authorization through payment of the appropriate per-copy fee to the Copyright Clearance Center, Inc., 222 Rosewood Drive, Danvers, MA 01923, (978) 750-8400, fax (978) 646-8600, or on the web at www.copyright.com. Requests to the Publisher for permission should be addressed to the Permissions Department, John Wiley & Sons, Inc., 111 River Street, Hoboken, NJ 07030, (201) 748-6011, fax (201) 748-6008, or online at http://www.wiley.com/go/permissions.

Limit of Liability/Disclaimer of Warranty: While the publisher and author have used their best efforts in preparing this book, they make no representations or warranties with respect to the accuracy or completeness of the contents of this book and specifically disclaim any implied warranties of merchantability or fitness for a particular purpose. No warranty may be created or extended by sales representatives or written sales materials. The advice and strategies contained herein may not be suitable for your situation. You should consult with a professional where appropriate. Neither the publisher nor author shall be liable for any loss of profit or any other commercial damages, including but not limited to special, incidental, consequential, or other damages.

For general information on our other products and services or for technical support, please contact our Customer Care Department within the United States at (800) 762-2974, outside the United States at (317) 572-3993 or fax (317) 572-4002.

Wiley also publishes its books in a variety of electronic formats. Some content that appears in print may not be available in electronic books. For more information about Wiley products, visit our website at www.wiley.com.

Library of Congress Cataloging-in-Publication Data:

Gordon, Jon, 1971-
 The seed : finding purpose and happiness in life and work / Jon Gordon.
  p. cm.
 Includes index.
 ISBN 978-0-470-88856-8 (hardback); ISBN 978-1-118-09024-4 (ebk);
 ISBN 978-1-118-09025-1 (ebk); ISBN 978-1-118-09026-8 (ebk)
  1. Work–Psychological aspects. 2. Conduct of life. 3. Inspiration. I. Title.
HF5548.8.G665 2011
650.1–dc22

2011012871

Printed in the United States of America
SKY10029275_082021

For Jade and Cole,

Be the Seed, do your best, and let God do the rest!

Contents

	Acknowledgments	*vii*
1	Two Weeks	1
2	Lost	5
3	A Higher Perspective	13
4	Dreams	19
5	On the Road to Find Out	23
6	Home	27
7	Happiness	33
8	Dharma	37
9	College	41
10	The One Song	43
11	Positive Point of View	49
12	Dogs Have a Purpose	55
13	The Restaurant	57
14	Service	63
15	Gifts from the Past	67

16	A New Opportunity	69
17	George	75
18	The Decision	87
19	GPT	89
20	The Purpose Process	91
21	Four Stages of Purpose	97
22	Y-Process	107
23	Stand Out	109
24	Growth	113
25	Tests	117
26	A Dream Remembered	121
27	Overcome	123
28	Making A Difference	125
29	A Name Means Something	127
30	Abundance	129
31	A Season for Everything	135
32	The Harvest	141
	Other Books by Jon Gordon	*145*

Acknowledgments

First, I want to thank my wife, Kathryn, for helping me find and live my purpose. I wouldn't be the man I am today if it weren't for you.

To my children Jade and Cole, thank you for your patience during the holidays as I wrote this book. Always remember to follow your passion and plant yourself where you are.

Thank you to my publisher, Matt Holt, and my editor, Shannon Vargo, and to Kim Dayman, Larry Olson, and the rest of the team at Wiley for helping me plant my seed and grow to my full potential. You are the best.

Thank you to my agent and marketing genius, Daniel Decker, for all your hard work, talent, and support. We are a great team.

Thank you to my brother, David Gordon, for your insights and encouragement as I wrote this book. Our creative brainstorming session while walking and talking made a huge difference in the writing of this book.

Thank you to Todd Gothberg, Dan Britton, Melissa Johnson, and Ben Newman for reading the manuscript, providing feedback, and challenging me to make it better.

Thank you to Paul and Alison Frase, for your faith and inspiration during the most painful time of your life. Joshua's legacy lives on, and he will be the catalyst for the cure of myotubular myopathy. You taught me the definition of *overcome* and Joshua taught me that we are not just another brick in the wall.

Thank you to all the seed planters out there who produce a harvest and make the world a better place. I hope you enjoy this book.

Most of all, I thank God for the inspiration to write this book. You have carried me through the biggest challenges of my life and taken me through the four stages of purpose. Thank you for using me for your purpose and for guiding me toward my purpose.

Chapter 1
Two Weeks

Josh cruised down the country road with his foot pressed firmly on the gas pedal. He loved driving with the radio up and the windows down. He wasn't sure who enjoyed it more—him or his dog, Dharma. With her head out the window and ears flapping, she seemed to relish the smell of the fresh country air even as the strong winds battered her face. Not a care in the world, Josh thought, as he looked over at her and shook his head. She doesn't have to worry about jobs and bosses and paychecks. She doesn't have to care about things like "engagement" or "focus" or "employment." Oh, to be so lucky.

They were miles from the city where Josh lived and worked—and far away from the challenges and concerns he faced. He wished he could just stick his head out the window and forget yesterday ever happened. He wished he could go back in time and take his father's advice. He wished he felt differently.

"I want to be you," Josh yelled to Dharma. Her ears perked up after hearing his voice. She turned toward him, letting her master know his words were more important than sunshine and fresh country air. Josh smiled at her. He was convinced she understood everything he said—whether they were taking a walk, going for a ride in the car, or sitting at home. She understood the creative ideas he shared while brainstorming in his "idea" room. She listened as he read books in bed and discussed life's biggest questions with her. She put her head in his lap when he shared his innermost and greatest fears. She not only knew his thoughts, she knew what was in his heart. As Josh approached his destination, he wished she could tell him what his heart was saying.

A sign on the side of the road let him know the farm where he was headed was only a few miles away. He was looking forward to seeing his friends. They had invited him to join them for a fun day. He had never been to a corn maze before and didn't know what to expect, but figured it had to be better than sitting at home feeling sorry for himself.

His friends knew what others did not. His life was not as perfect as it seemed. Sure, he had a great place to live, a great job with a well-respected company, and a bright future. Yet something was missing. He was no longer excited to go to work. It wasn't that Josh hated his job. It was just that he didn't love it anymore. And everyone knew it, including his boss, who had called Josh into his office yesterday, on a Friday of all days, to break the news.

"You're not the same guy I hired five years ago," his boss, Mark, had said. "You had the fire in your belly. You were passionate and full of ideas and energy. Now it seems you don't even want to be here anymore. What's up?"

Josh looked down at the ground, not wanting to look his boss in the eye. He knew Mark was right, but hearing him say the truth made everything more real. He felt exposed and ashamed. "I don't know," Josh said as he looked up and shook his head. "I wish I had an answer, but I don't. I'm just not feeling it lately. I don't know why. I'm just not." He wasn't sure whether he should have told the truth, but his upbringing and his own experience told him an honest answer was always the best answer. Besides, he wore the truth on his face every day, and his body language over the past year spoke volumes.

"Well, you know that passion is a big part of what we do," his boss said. If we don't have passion, then we are like everyone else—mediocre—and that's not good enough for me, our company, or our clients.

"Am I being fired?" Josh asked. He always remembered when he was twelve years old and had broken his arm; the doctor had walked in, looked at the X-ray, then immediately grabbed his arm and made small talk. Next, without any warning—*crack*—the doctor had set his broken bone back in place. Ever since, Josh believed in getting painful or uncomfortable moments over with as quickly as possible.

"No," Mark replied, shaking his head, "I'm not ready to give up on you yet. We've invested way too much in you to just let you go, and I believe you've invested too much in us to give up now. I've seen this before, and I think you need a break. So here's the deal: I'm giving you two weeks. Think of it as a reverse two weeks' notice. Instead of being fired after two weeks, my hope is that you'll be rehired. Sort of like a fresh start. You have two paid weeks off to decide whether you really, truly, and passionately want to be here. If, after two weeks, you decide this is not right for you, I'll be disappointed, but at least we'll both know it's time to move on and not go through the motions any longer. It's simple. You either want to be here and give 110 percent, or you find something else you want to do that, hopefully, will light the spark you once had here."

"Deal?" Mark asked as he reached out to shake Josh's hand. "Deal," Josh replied, as he shook his boss's hand and walked out the door, wondering whether he should be cheering or crying. While most people would love a paid two-week vacation to decide their future, for Josh there was nothing more frightening.

Chapter 2

Lost

Josh recalled the previous day's conversation with his boss as he drove through the entrance to the farm and felt the same knot in his stomach. It would have been easier being fired, he thought. At least the decision would have been made for him. It occurred to him that today, Saturday, was the first day of his two-week vacation before he would have to give an answer to his boss. He would have to make a decision by then, but not today. Today he didn't want to make any decisions. Today he just wanted to put everything out of his mind and have some fun.

The farm was larger than he'd expected. Giant stalks of corn seemed to grow everywhere along the long, winding road Josh navigated to get to the farmhouse and entrance to the corn maze. He arrived at the farmhouse, parked his car, laid out a blanket for Dharma to lie on for a nap, and cracked the car window for her so she could enjoy the cool October country air. Then he paid for his ticket and ran to greet his friends, who were waiting for him at the entrance to the maze. On his way, he passed a line of people waiting their turn to board a propeller plane to see the maze and the countryside from the air. Not on your life, Josh thought. The only planes I fly are jets with pilots and flight attendants who serve peanuts, pretzels, and drinks.

Josh found his friends, and they exchanged hugs, high fives, and handshakes. After making bets about who would get through the maze first, they lined up to begin the race. It didn't take long for Josh and his friends to lose each other, since the maze offered many dead ends, forks, paths, and choices. When faced with a choice of two paths, some chose one path while others chose another. This continued until, eventually, the group was completely divided and Josh was alone and lost in the maze.

Ever since he'd been a kid, Josh had had a fear of getting lost, and, as he stood facing a wall of cornstalks, he became increasingly anxious. Should he take the path to the left or to the right? Should he go backward and take a different path? Should he shout to his friends? He closed his eyes to pray for direction, and when he opened them, he saw a tall, lanky, old farmer with long gray hair and a gray mustache standing in front of him. Startled, Josh nervously asked where he had come from.

"Oh, I came from the maze," the farmer said with a raspy voice. "This is my farm, and I like to walk the maze and help people who are lost find their way."

"That's great," Josh said, feeling more at ease, "I'm definitely lost. Can you help me?"

"That remains to be seen," the farmer replied. "First, can you tell me where you are going?"

"Well, I'm trying to get to the end of the maze," Josh said, thinking the farmer's question was weird and the answer obvious: "If I knew where I were going, I'd be there by now."

The farmer took a deep breath and smiled, "Josh, I'm not talking about the maze. I'm talking about life. Do you know where you are going with your life?"

Josh looked around nervously and thought, "How does he know my name?" He looked for his friends and the hidden camera. Surely his friends were playing a trick on him. They knew he was going through a crisis, and perhaps they were doing something radical to slap him out of his funk. What better way than a practical joke? He called to his friends, and when no one came out from the cornstalks he felt strange.

"You didn't answer the question," the farmer said, as he stared at Josh with a slight grin on his face, "Do you know where you are going with your life?"

Josh took a small step backwards.

"How do you know my name, and why are you asking me this?" Josh asked forcefully, becoming more uncomfortable.

"I know everyone who comes through this maze," the farmer said reassuringly. "I've found enough lost people to know when they are lost, and you, my friend, are as lost as they come. But don't worry about it. Millions of people are lost like you. Many come to the maze in search of something. They come from all professions, all backgrounds, and all ages. Some are in search of their dream job. Some just want to find a little fun and happiness in their life. Some are looking for more meaning in their work. Others are facing some kind of adversity and are filled with uncertainty and fear. They're searching for answers and wish someone would tell them what to do next. But then they meet me and I explain that the maze offers the lessons to create the life they want. As I said, I help people find their way. If you listen to me, I'll not only help you find your way out of the maze, I'll help you find direction for your life."

Josh scanned the old man's face. There was a calm, peaceful presence about him. He figured the farmer had learned his name from the booth where he had paid for his ticket and signed up for the mailing list. If the old man could help Josh get out of the maze, he was all ears. Direction for his life, however, was not on his list of priorities at the moment.

"Okay, I'm listening."

"You're lost because you don't know your purpose!" the farmer exclaimed. "Purpose is our ultimate guidance system that provides us with direction for our lives. Purpose fuels us with passion, and this passion gives us confidence and vitality to go after our dreams. To live without purpose is to wander aimlessly through life like dust in the wind. You become one of the walking dead, meandering among the living. But when you find your purpose, you discover the power that fuels all of creation. You find your reason for existing. You find the path you were meant to travel and the passion to thrive on your journey."

"And where do I find this purpose?" Josh asked. After hearing words like *passion* and *purpose*, he was now more interested in what the farmer had to say. Just the other night, he had closed his eyes and asked to be able to know and live his purpose. It was a simple prayer he hadn't said in a long time. "Use me for your purpose. Guide me toward my purpose." And now, here he was, having a conversation about purpose with a stranger in a corn maze. He should have known better. Like the title of one of his favorite songs, he knew God moves in mysterious ways.

"I thought I'd found my purpose," Josh added, "when I got my first job after college. Now, though, I'm questioning everything: my job, my past decisions, my future. You're absolutely right, I am lost."

"Well you don't have to be lost anymore," the farmer said, as he grabbed a seed from his pocket and handed it to Josh. Josh looked at the seed while it rested in the palm of his hand. "What is this for?" he asked.

The farmer paused for a moment, pointed at the seed, and said, "Find out where to plant this seed and your purpose will be revealed to you."

Josh looked at the seed skeptically. "How can planting this seed help reveal my purpose?"

"I'm not sure how it works," the farmer responded, "I just know it works. It's one of those mysteries of life—where our belief in miracles allows us to see more miracles and where our imagination somehow creates our reality. I've given seeds to hundreds of people, and they have discovered their purpose. They all come back to tell me so, and I hope you will do the same when you find yours."

"What happens if I don't try to find out where to plant the seed?" Josh asked, hoping there was another option he could try.

"Then you won't find your purpose," the farmer answered, knowing there was only one way. "Everyone must embark on a quest to find their purpose. It's the one thing in life that truly matters, and if you don't pursue it, everything else is meaningless. The journey is not easy. It's filled with mystery, challenges, obstacles, and dead ends—much like this maze. But if you are willing to follow the path and learn from wrong turns and keep moving forward, even when you want to give up, you will eventually find the right place to plant your seed."

"Where do I start?" Josh asked curiously. "I have no idea where to begin."

"Begin where all knowing exists. Begin with your heart. And be careful of your mind. It will often play tricks on you and deceive you on your quest. But your heart never lies. It knows your *why*. It knows where you are meant to go and what you are meant to do. You just have to listen to it. And while you are following your heart, also look for the signs."

"What signs?" Josh asked, knowing his heart certainly wasn't forthcoming with information lately.

"The signs of grace that guide you through life," the farmer explained. "These signs help you decide which roads to take. They come in many forms: advice from a stranger, dreams, eureka moments, songs, television shows, books, and even big signs on the side of the road. God uses all means to communicate with us to guide us on our journey.

If we are open to these signs, look for them, and follow them, they will guide us in the right direction. The more we look for and believe in the signs the more they appear."

Josh smiled. He knew about signs. His father had always talked about them, and Josh had seen them throughout his life. When he would walk on the beach as a teenager, he would ask for a sign and, sure enough, a flock of seagulls would fly overhead at that moment. He often saw 11:11 and 1:11 on clocks and his phone and whenever he did he knew it was going to be a great day. It happened too many times to chalk it up to coincidence. Signs had helped Josh make some of the most important decisions in his life. Lately, however, he had forgotten they existed and had stopped looking for them.

The farmer continued, "A quest for your purpose is like a cosmic game, and once you know how to play and embrace the game, it becomes an exciting adventure."

The words *adventure* and *game* stuck in Josh's mind. He used to think of life as an adventure. He used to see it as a gift, not an obligation. Lately, though, it didn't feel like a game. It felt like a homework assignment. And, although he believed in what the farmer was saying, he wasn't sure he had the energy or desire to play the game or embark on an adventure.

"If you don't feel like playing the game," the famer said, as if reading Josh's mind, "or if you feel like giving up after the game starts because the search seems futile, remember this: The fact that you have a desire to search for your purpose means there is a purpose to be found. Why else would you and so many people be searching for it? The fact that you seek it means it exists. So, play the game, Josh, and don't give up. Follow your heart and follow the signs, and you will find where to plant the seed." And then the farmer added with a big smile, "Oh, and there's one more thing you must know before I leave you."

"What's that?" Josh asked, expecting to hear more profound advice.

"To get out of the maze, take this path to the right, follow it, and it will bring you to the exit. I've got to go help a few more people who are lost. Remember to come back and see me," he shouted as he disappeared down the path to the left.

Chapter 3

A Higher Perspective

It's not every day someone tells you that you can find your purpose by planting a seed. It sounded strange to Josh, and he knew it would sound even weirder to his friends. They were already concerned about him, and he didn't want them to think he was losing it, so Josh decided to not tell his friends about his encounter with the farmer.

They spent the rest of the afternoon enjoying hay rides, carving pumpkins, and relaxing on rocking chairs by the farmhouse. Even Dharma had a great time running around the farm. Hoping to have one last conversation with the old farmer, Josh waited around until all his friends had gone. With the farmer nowhere to be found and only a few hours of daylight left, Josh knew it was time to get back to the city, so he and Dharma headed toward the car. Along the way they passed the pilot and the propeller plane. The line of people was gone, but the smell of gasoline remained.

"You want the last flight of the night?" the pilot asked as Josh passed her. "Perfect time for flying. The sky is clear. The air is crisp. It doesn't get much better than this."

"No thanks. We have to get back to the city," Josh answered as he rubbed Dharma's head.

"Your dog can come, too," the pilot responded. "There's room enough for both of you. And besides, one ride with me and you'll find what you are looking for."

Josh stopped dead in his tracks. Was she a friend of the farmer's? Or was she just a good saleswoman looking to make another buck? "How do you know I'm looking for something?" Josh asked.

"Everybody's looking for something. Love, money, happiness. We're all looking for something. And when you are up in the sky with me, whatever it is you are looking for becomes a lot clearer. Once you see the world the way I see it, you'll never see things the same way again. So, what is it that you are looking for?" the pilot asked.

"My purpose." Josh decided to just throw it out there for shock effect. "Can you help me see that more clearly?" he asked sarcastically.

"Well, yes, I can," the pilot answered. "Hop in and see for yourself."

Josh wasn't sure if it was what she said or the way she said it, but something compelled him to jump into the plane. Never in his wildest dreams did he think he would get in a plane like this, and yet here he was, about to take off, with Dharma excitedly fidgeting next to him. As the pilot started the engine and began to gain speed along the dusty runway, she looked back at Josh and Dharma. "Yep, when you're searching for your purpose, sometimes the best thing you can do is take a break, levitate, and gain a new perspective."

With his eyes closed and his heart pounding, Josh could feel the plane climb higher in the sky. He could hear the annoying high-pitched sound of the engine and feel the chill of the air against his face as the vibration caused by the propeller made his body hum along with the plane. He wanted to open his eyes, but he couldn't. He not only had a fear of heights, he had a fear of being on a small plane when the engine dies. He had a fear of crashing into a million pieces.

"You can't gain a new perspective with your eyes closed," the pilot shouted. "And you'll never find your purpose if you don't open your eyes. It's amazing how many people go through life with their eyes closed," she thought. "They allow fear to blind them, and they miss all the miracles, beauty, and opportunities around them."

Josh shook his head, knowing the pilot was right. He was allowing his fear to get the best of him, and if there was one thing he prided himself on, it was facing his fears. He forced himself to open his eyes, and when he did he saw before him the most spectacular sunset he'd ever seen. Never in his life had the sun appeared so big, so red, and so beautiful. It was as if someone had painted it for him and if he reached out his arm he could touch it. "Isn't it beautiful!" he exclaimed to Dharma, who loved air travel more than car rides. He looked toward the front of the plane and saw nothing but blue skies and a few sparse clouds. He looked down and could see the maze. He could see the entrance, the twists and turns, including the section where he'd become lost and the exit where he had escaped. It all looked so small, so easy. He laughed at himself for feeling anxious when he had been lost. "Wow. It looks so different from up here," he shouted to the pilot. "I got lost in the maze today, but now I can clearly see where I got stuck and the path I should have taken."

"I told you so," shouted the pilot. "Everything becomes clearer up here. I love my job, because every time I fly above the maze I'm reminded of the way God sees us and the world. Similar to your view of the maze from the plane, God sees your beginning, middle, and end. You may feel lost, but God knows where you began, where you are now, and where you are supposed to go. The big picture is clear when you see things from a higher perspective.

"Now if I could only maintain this higher perspective while in the maze of life," Josh shouted.

"You can," responded the pilot, "and when you do, you can move forward with faith, knowing there is a path that will take you to your destination. You just have to ask for guidance to take you there."

Josh thought of the farmer who provided the guidance that helped him find the right path out of the maze. Perhaps in finding direction for his life, he needed to ask for more guidance. The farmer said to look for the signs, but what happens when the signs aren't always clear? What do you do when you ask for guidance yet don't receive an answer and feel like you're running through life alone? He looked at the maze and thought of his purpose. He saw the maze from a different perspective, but his purpose wasn't any clearer. He had no clue where to plant the seed, and he wasn't sure how looking at the maze would help him decide. He shouted to the pilot, "I love what you are saying, but you said that if I took a ride with you I'd see my purpose more clearly; so far, it's not looking any clearer."

The pilot laughed. Years of flying and meditating on higher thoughts and perspectives had inspired her to see things that others did not. "Look at the maze again," she shouted, "From up here, you realize that in life, as in the maze, your beginning, end, and the journey in between are all connected. Your past leads to your future, and your future is connected to your past. You can't have one without the other. To see your purpose more clearly, you have to go backward in order to move forward. Think about your past and you'll find the clues to create your future."

"I don't get it," Josh shouted as the pilot began to prepare the plane for landing. "How can my past help me know my purpose?"

"Let me land the plane and I'll explain," the pilot shouted.

After a smooth landing and a sigh of relief from Josh, they hopped out of the plane. Dharma stood by Josh's side as the pilot shared a story to help Josh understand.

"I read an article about a celebrity host of a television show. When she was young, she loved entertaining people and making them laugh. As the years passed, she listened more to what others thought she should do with her life rather than listening to her own heart and passion. It wasn't until she was 40 years old and a high school teacher that she realized she was the funny one at all the parties. She started to do stand-up comedy, and this led to her current purpose and passion-filled life in show business. When asked about her journey and the lessons she'd learned, she said that when it comes to goals, people should do the things they loved to do when they were 10 years old—an age before we start caring about what others think.

"You see, your past provides clues about your passion. Go to your past, and you will find direction for your future."

Chapter 4

Dreams

Sleep had never been a problem for Josh. Years of working through the night to finish sales and marketing campaigns had prepared his body to sleep anytime, anywhere. When he slept, he slept so hard nothing woke him up. But that night, he was awakened by the simple touch of Dharma's tongue licking his hand. He looked at the seed on his nightstand and remembered the strange dream he had just been having. In the dream he planted the seed in a pot on his desk, and the seed became a plant that grew too large to keep in his office. So he took the plant out of the pot and planted it in a big field, where he and a group of people watched it rise steadily while fruit started falling off the tree. Josh turned to the people in the dream and shouted, "I know what it means. I know what it means." But before he could reveal the answer, Dharma woke him up.

He grabbed the seed on his nightstand and walked to the window. From there he could see and feel the pulse of the city. Even at 2 a.m., the downtown streets were filled with people and cars. They're not just running through the city. They're running through life, he thought. I bet most of them don't have a clue about their purpose. They don't think about it or seek it. They scurry from one place to the next. They live paycheck to paycheck. They engage in the daily fight for survival. He knew them well because he had become just like them, until his boss's ultimatum and his conversation with the farmer and pilot prompted him to examine his life.

Now he couldn't stop thinking about seeds and purpose. He wondered whether it was better to race through life feeling numb to your purpose or to experience the discomfort and struggle of seeking it. He thought about his job and his lack of passion and decided he didn't have a choice. Although it was easier being numb, that was no longer an option for him. He would rather have a meaningful life than an easy life. He looked at the seed in his hand. The farmer might be crazy, but Josh had had stranger conversations and witnessed crazier things in his life, so he did not discount him completely. Besides, he had plenty of time on his hands, and he would use this time to embrace the game and try to figure out where to plant the seed. An adventure was the last thing he wanted, but he knew that life doesn't always give you what you want. It gives you what you need.

He had nothing to lose, and perhaps if he found where to plant the seed, he would find his purpose, and his purpose would also help him decide whether he wanted to stay in his job or move on. His boss needed an answer, and Josh needed to find his purpose.

He grabbed a suitcase, filled it with clothes, grabbed Dharma's things, and he and his dog walked to the car. He had decided to go back home to the town where he grew up. He didn't know whether he was supposed to plant the seed there, but he figured it would be a good place to start . . .

Because your past provides clues to your future.

Because he wanted to talk to his parents.

Because he honestly didn't know where else to go.

Chapter 5

On the Road to Find Out

 Josh hated driving next to large trucks on the highways, but unfortunately there were many on the road. Driving in the middle of the night reminded him of the many road trips he had taken with his band during the summers of high school and college. It wasn't a great band, but it was good, and Josh was the lead singer and guitarist. He had developed his craft as a young worship leader in his dad's church. His family had hoped he would join his family in ministry, but Josh had felt pulled in a different direction, first to the music world and then to the business world.

Josh had friends who had become coaches because their dad had been a coach or who had gone into business because their dad was in business, but Josh had the desire to do something different—something he could call his own. He didn't think it was wrong for people to follow their parents and siblings into the family business, especially if it was something they loved to do, but he knew there was something else for him. It wasn't that he didn't love the ministry, either. Being a worship leader had been one of the most special times in his life. He loved ministry and was very good at it. He could not only sing and play music, but he was also a great communicator. He loved making a difference and inspiring people. He loved helping his father develop creative ideas for sermons. He loved the immediate feedback he received about his talks and songs. That's why everyone was shocked when he made the decision to pursue a life outside of the church.

As Josh thought about his past and drove with the radio blaring and the windows down, he wondered if he had made the wrong decision. He thought of the story the pilot had told him about doing what you loved to do when you were 10. He thought about his strengths and gifts, and they pointed toward ministry. Yet when he had graduated from college and his father had asked him to be his church's full-time worship leader, Josh answered that in his heart he knew it wasn't the life for him. It felt too comfortable—too safe. He wanted to work in business and engage the marketplace with his gifts and passion. His father supported his decision, and after a brief stint as a musician, Josh ultimately chose a career in business. Taking a job that initially excited and challenged him, he joined a company where he felt he could make his mark. But after a few years, the newness wore off. His passion for creating new sales and marketing campaigns gave way to the pressure of meeting deadlines and the stress of hitting the targeted numbers and goals. His desire to engage the marketplace was now replaced by doubts about whether he was making a difference in the world other than making more money for his company.

"I know I'm here for a reason, aren't I, girl?" Josh said to Dharma, who was not only listening to the words he said but also to the thoughts that ran through his mind. Josh had told Dharma he was convinced she knew what he was saying and thinking, and he was right! She understood his thoughts, words, and feelings. She knew when he was coming home from work and when they would be going for a walk or a ride in the car. It wasn't because she had learned Josh's habits. He was a spontaneous person and had a varied schedule. She knew these things because she knew the future before it happened. Humans call it a sixth sense. For her it was simply Dog Sense. She was much smarter and knew a lot more than people realized, but it was a good thing to be underestimated. She licked Josh's arm to let him know he was loved. She knew comfort was what he needed most right now.

"We'll figure it out," Josh said as he rubbed her head and sped past three large trucks. They had been on the road for a while, and as the moon gave way to the sun, and darkness surrendered to light, Josh was filled with a lot of questions. As he neared his destination, he just hoped his father would help him with some answers.

Chapter 6

Home

There's nothing like a mother's hug. It has the power to take away your pain and fear and to comfort you during the most difficult times. One hug and you feel as though everything is going to be okay. As Josh hugged his mom at the front door, with tears flowing down both of their faces, he once again felt like the boy who was lost at the mall but eventually found. She hugged him now as she had hugged him then. Josh hadn't told her what was going on in his life, but he didn't have to. A mom just knows.

She grabbed him by the hand, took him into the kitchen, and made him a hearty breakfast while they talked about his challenges. The rest of the family was already at church, getting ready for Sunday services. Josh took a long, hot shower, put on some fresh clothes, and hopped in the car with his mom to join the rest of the family.

It had been six months since he had last been home to attend his father's church, but the minute he stepped into the building it felt like he'd been there yesterday. He marveled at his father's energy and ability to inspire people despite sharing the same message during three different services. He spoke at 9:00 a.m., 10:30 a.m., and 5:00 p.m., yet his last sermon was delivered as powerfully and passionately as the first. Josh noted that his oldest brother was also a powerful force when he spoke. His brother, who had a heart for helping the homeless, sick, and poor around the world, encouraged people to get involved and explained all the ways people could make a difference: He talked about building wells in Africa to provide clean drinking water for people; helping families hit hard by the economy; feeding hundreds of homeless people each week at the church; and the outreach initiative to visit community members who needed support, encouragement, and someone to talk to.

Josh couldn't help but feel small. His brother was doing so much. What was he doing to help people? What difference was he making? People were homeless, hungry, and sick, and here he was, worried about whether he should stay in his job or not. At least he had a job and a choice. What choice did some of these people have? He remembered a line from a poem:

I had the blues because I had no shoes
until upon the street I met a man that had no feet.

Later that evening, Josh sat with his dad in the study. His brothers had returned to their homes with their families, and his parent's house was quiet except for the sound of his mother cooking in the kitchen. His dad was surprised but thrilled to see him.

"So, what brought you home?" his dad asked with a big smile on his face. "Is everything okay?"

Josh told him about the conversations he had had with his boss, with the farmer who gave him the seed, and with the pilot who'd told him to find clues in his past. Josh knew his dad wouldn't find anything strange about this string of events. Years of being a pastor had taught him that truth is stranger than fiction. He heard all sorts of stories and saw all kinds of things that made him a believer in forces beyond our five senses. He found that what was unseen was more powerful than what you could see, and he believed that miracles didn't just happen 2,000 years ago but were happening on earth right now.

His dad paused as he reflected on what his son told him. He then walked over to the book shelf. "If there's one thing I know, it's that following your purpose often requires a change in your life, and God will use all sorts of people and situations to bring about this change. It's clear you met these people for a reason, Josh, and I'm thinking that you need to accept this challenge and go find where to plant the seed. As I always told you, God doesn't choose the best. God chooses the most willing. If you are willing to seek your purpose and God with your whole heart God will do amazing things with your life."

"I am willing and committed Dad," Josh answered, nodding in agreement. "I just have no idea where to plant it. I wish someone would give me the answer. I wish I knew how it all plays out."

"Well, my son, if you knew all the answers and how things would play out, then there'd be no point in going for the ride. It wouldn't be an adventure if you knew everything that was going to happen. It's the adventure that makes you stronger, wiser, and better. This journey is part of your destiny!"

"But maybe my journey is supposed to start and end right here," Josh said. "Maybe I'm supposed to plant the seed here at the ministry with you. Maybe this is my purpose."

Josh's dad put his hand on his shoulder. "While I'd love nothing more, I can't expect you to live my dream. You have to live your dream. Sure, I was a little disappointed when you first told me you'd decided to pursue a career in business instead of the ministry. But I've since come to peace with your decision, knowing it was the right one. Too many people don't pursue their purpose and passion in life because they choose to conform to the pressure and expectations of those around them. They also listen to the naysayers and impossibility thinkers instead of to their own hearts. To find your calling, you have to overcome all these outside forces that attempt to hold you back. You have chosen to do this, and I couldn't be more proud of you. I don't know where you are supposed to plant the seed, but I know it's not here. I also know that you are meant to go on this journey because there's something more for you to do. You're not happy where you are for a reason. And I believe that when you find out where to plant the seed, those reasons will be very clear to you. I also know that there are no accidents, and you, my son, are not an accident and neither am I."

Josh was comforted by his father's words. He had always felt as though he was here to do something special, yet lately his fear and doubts were making him feel very insignificant. His dad, however, thought differently.

"The other day I was reading an article about our planet, and it said that Earth is really a giant sphere made of mostly hot liquid and that it's spinning approximately 1,000 miles per hour while traveling around the sun at approximately 66,000 miles per hour. That's 1.2 million frequent-flier miles a day," he said as Josh laughed. "Also consider that Earth is about 93 million miles from the sun. Any closer and it would be too hot to sustain life. Any farther and it would be too cold to sustain life. It's all too perfect. Our existence didn't come about by accident because the conditions were right. The right conditions were created on purpose to provide for our existence. We are here for a purpose. I have one. You have one. Everyone has one. And the fact that you are searching for it couldn't make me happier."

Josh hugged his dad. He had always had the gift of making everything so clear, attainable, and doable. Now Josh just had to find the energy to do it. He said good night to his dad, then walked into the kitchen to kiss his mother good night. Ignoring the delicious aroma of her home cooking, he and Dharma walked upstairs to his bedroom.

He was too tired to eat and too exhausted to say another word. He fell into his bed with his clothes on and looked at the pictures on his wall. They were memories from his past, but they were not to be part of his future. He wasn't meant to plant the seed at home. He was meant to go on a journey. Now he just had to figure out where to go next.

Chapter 7

Happiness

The next morning Josh sat on the couch enjoying his magazine. He felt refreshed after a great night's sleep and a hearty breakfast. His parents were taking a walk, and he and Dharma had the house to themselves. Josh was prone to read all sorts of magazines and newspapers, having discovered that the articles often led to random insights and creative ideas for his work. One time he'd read an article about a small business called Taco Truck out of New Jersey that was using social media to connect with its customers. This inspired Josh to spearhead an initiative to help his company communicate better both internally and externally. He never knew where his next idea would come from, and it was one of the aspects about his job that still excited him.

As he turned the pages, Dharma unexpectedly hopped up from where she was lying and pressed her nose in the magazine. At first, Josh thought she was trying to get into his lap, but then realized she was moving the pages with her nose. After turning the pages to the middle of the magazine, she resumed her place by Josh's feet and rested her head on his shoes. Yes, dogs know more than humans think. When Josh looked down at the magazine, he noticed it was an article about happiness and how all sorts of companies were using happiness in their marketing messages. "Okay, girl, if you want me to read this I will," he said, patting her head as she licked his hand.

The article talked about how all these companies were selling "happiness," and yet so few people were actually happy at work. I can relate, Josh thought. "I guess you want me to be happier," he said to Dharma, and then wondered if he was as happy as she was. The answer was clearly no. And Josh wondered whether he had *ever* been as happy as Dharma.

Yes. The answer came from deep within.

But when? he asked himself.

In that moment the television turned on. How this happened he had no idea, since the remote was on the table a few feet from them. But it turned on, and what Josh saw made it clear that it was a sign meant for him. It was his favorite movie from his college days. He must have watched it 10 times and knew every word. He remembered sitting around the television in his college apartment with his friends, watching the movie and thinking, "It doesn't get any better than this."

He turned to Dharma. "Yes, I was as happy as you once," he said. "I was happy when I was in college. Maybe I should plant the seed there." He said the words without thinking, but when he heard himself say them, he felt an energy course through his body as a series of thoughts filled his mind:

> *Dharma turning the magazine to the article on happiness*
> *Questions of his own happiness*
> *The movie from college reminding him of a time he'd been happy*
> *The farmer telling him to look for the signs*

He rubbed Dharma's belly while she playfully rolled around on the floor. He was more energized than he had been in a long time. He knew where he was supposed to plant the seed. It all made sense. He was supposed to plant the seed where he had been happiest, and he had been happiest in college. "Find where you were happy, and you'll find the clues to reveal your purpose." Maybe I'm even supposed to be a teacher or professor, Josh thought. He could hardly wait. He packed up his clothes and waited for his parents to return home from their walk. After telling them about his revelation, he and Dharma ran to the car and took off for another long drive to visit his college.

Chapter 8

Dharma

Dharma once again enjoyed the smell of fresh air pummeling her face. She was getting the opportunity to smell all kinds of smells from many different places. She was also listening to all of Josh's favorite songs. It was an eclectic mix of music: classical, pop, hard rock, classic rock, and country. Josh liked it all, and the music gave him ideas for creating his own songs. When he listened to songs that contained bad words or negative phrases, he changed the lyrics as he sang them to Dharma. For instance, when he sang one of his favorite songs, "Another Brick in the Wall," he would sing, "You're *not* just another brick in the wall." Simply adding the word *not* changed the meaning of the entire song.

Dharma loved the meaning of songs. That's why country music was her favorite. She liked the stories the songs told. Most people thought country music told sad stories about people losing everything, including their dogs, but actually many of the songs were very uplifting. Dharma's favorite song was "Live Like You Were Dying," by Tim McGraw. She knew humans needed to make the most of life and enjoy the one ride they had. It's why she didn't mind that Josh drove fast along the highway.

Ever since Josh had read a book to her about a dog that could talk and his owner, a race-car driver, she had an appreciation for dogs that could communicate and masters who drove fast cars. Josh didn't know it, but in her mind she was saying, "Faster, faster." She cared less about where they were going than he did. It was the *ride* that Dharma loved. She knew Josh should have been tired of driving by now, but he wasn't. She could feel his excitement about visiting his college for the first time in five years. She could hear the happiness in his voice as he turned down the music and shared with her all his favorite memories from college. She listened intently, knowing that it made him feel good to talk.

Josh told her about all his favorite places at college where he could possibly plant the seed. He talked about the bench outside his freshman dorm where he had spent a lot of time studying. He considered the yard outside his fraternity house where he had made friends for life. He had spent countless hours out there playing football, talking about future goals, and playing music at parties. He also contemplated the spot on the field where he had received his diploma during graduation. They were all good places, but Josh didn't think they felt quite right.

Then, after a few minutes of silence, Josh told Dharma exactly where he was supposed to plant the seed. It was his favorite place and held his happiest memories. It was in the field outside the lecture hall that housed his favorite class and favorite professor. The class was music history, and the professor didn't just lecture—he told stories; he entertained; he shared lessons for life. Each lecture had a purpose, and Josh loved them. The class was so popular that there was a waiting list to get in. In addition to loving the class, Josh also loved spending time before the class playing his guitar in the field under a tree. Other students would gather around and listen to him. With a guitar, a song, and an audience, Josh was as happy as could be. Yes, this was the place to plant the seed.

If she could have talked, she would have told him whether his choice was the correct one. But perhaps that's why dogs can't talk. It's because they know things before they happen. They know things that humans are not supposed to know yet. They know things that humans are meant to figure out for themselves. If dogs shared what they knew, it would ruin the experience humans were meant to go through in order to become better people.

Dharma's job was to help nudge and guide Josh in the right direction and to love him unconditionally when he made mistakes. She knew where he was supposed to plant the seed, but it wasn't her purpose to tell him. He would have to figure it out for himself.

Chapter 9
College

You can never step in the same river twice. Life is always changing and flowing. This was never more obvious than when Josh and Dharma walked around his college campus. He had been gone for only five years, yet there were new buildings and construction everywhere. It was late October and the smell of the air let Dharma know that the seasons were about to change. For Josh, the air was also filled with the buzz and excitement of students enjoying the time of their lives. Together, they walked around to see the sights of all his favorite places. They walked to his freshman dorm and to his fraternity house. He showed her the various buildings where he had taken classes. "You never got to see these places before," Josh told her, as he recalled his college girlfriend giving Dharma to him as a graduation present. It was their last day on campus. She'd handed the dog to him in a box and said her name was Dharma. When he opened the box, he saw the cutest thing in the world, and he knew he had a best friend for life. "It's good to be back, isn't it, girl?" he asked, and his temperature rose when he showed Dharma the place where he and his college girlfriend had kissed for the first time while watching the sunset. Each building and location told a story and brought back many great memories and feelings.

Josh was as happy as could be . . . until he and Dharma came to the area where he was planning to plant the seed. *"Noooo!"* he shouted.

It was painfully evident that a large new building had been built on the very spot where he had entertained his fellow students before class. His happy place had been covered with concrete and replaced by classrooms, lecture halls, and offices.

Dharma licked his hand to let him know she sympathized with his frustration. Yes, life is always changing. Yes, sometimes humans need to figure things out for themselves.

"What do I do now, girl?" he said rubbing her head. "Maybe there's another place on campus where I'm supposed to plant the seed. Or maybe this is a sign that I'm not supposed to plant the seed at college." He didn't know what to think. He never thought there would be as good of an alternative. He had been happiest in college, so this *had* to be the place. "Now what?" he shouted as he looked at the building where he had taken his favorite class with his favorite professor. "Come on, let's go see if he's here." His former professor was one of the wisest people he knew, and wisdom was something he desperately needed right now.

Chapter 10
The One Song

They climbed the stairs to the second floor of the building and found his former professor, Mr. Goldman, sitting in the same small, cluttered office he had occupied five years earlier. Some things in life don't change after all—especially offices of brilliant but crazy college professors. To Dharma, he smelled like a nice man. To Josh, he hadn't changed a bit—except for having less hair on his balding head and a rounder face. Mr. Goldman's face lit up when he saw Josh. "How's my favorite student?" he asked cheerfully.

"Great," said Josh, "How's my favorite professor?"

"Doing well," Mr. Goldman answered, "Getting older, but getting better, as I always say. You know, I was thinking about you the other day and wondering how you were doing and what you were up to."

"Funny you should ask," said Josh. "That's why I came back here. Just trying to figure some things out." Then Josh tried changing the subject by asking, "Are you still teaching the same classes?" Josh felt embarrassed that his life hadn't yet amounted to much.

"Same classes but different lessons. You know me. I'm always trying to tweak my lectures to keep things fresh. If I taught the same lessons the same way, I'd not only put the class to sleep, I'd fall asleep myself. I'm actually working on some really exciting new lessons. Since I'm teaching music history, I had the idea that I should start from the beginning of music."

When was that?" Josh asked.

"All the way back in the beginning," Mr. Goldman said with a chuckle. "I came across a beautifully written article about the music of the spheres. It is believed that if one is looking for the origin of music, one must look to the sky, to the celestial bodies in the universe—to the sun, moon, and planets—that create a form of music as they orbit in space. While this music isn't audible to the naked ear, according to various religions, the spheres create a form of harmonic cosmic and spiritual music. In Buddhism, for example, it is believed that through extensive meditation people can reach a higher state of consciousness that allows them to hear this music, whereas Jewish tradition believes the music of the spheres offers the cosmos a way of praising the creator.

"This gave me all sorts of ideas, and it occurred to me that the word *universe* literally means *one song*. We are living in the one song. As we know music doesn't happen by accident. It is arranged into notes and patterns to create certain vibrations and sounds through a creative process. Just as the music you or I create is an expression of us, the one song is an expression of the ultimate creator. All music begins here. Music history matters more than I realized, and music exists for a purpose greater than I could have imagined."

"Wow. I never thought about music like that," Josh said, still wishing he knew the greater purpose for which he existed.

"So, what are you trying to figure out?" Mr. Goldman asked, as if on cue. Dharma wasn't the only one who could sense his desperation, and the professor knew that students came back to their college for one of two reasons: Either they were feeling nostalgic or they were lost.

Josh told him about his job and his boss's ultimatum. He didn't tell him about the farmer or the seed, but he did share the questions he had about his purpose and his thoughts about teaching, possibly even becoming a college professor.

"I can't tell you whether being a teacher or professor is right for you, Josh." Dharma looked up. She knew the answer but remained silent. "But I can tell you," Mr. Goldman continued, "that if you are looking for your purpose, college is probably not the place where you'll find it. While a few do, most people don't find their purpose in college. Rather, college is a place that prepares you for your purpose. It's where you transition from being a kid to an adult. College helps you decide what you like and don't like. It's a place where you find your autonomy and yourself. So, I think a better question to ask right now is this: How did college prepare you to live your purpose? And, to answer, ask yourself one more question: What did you love about college?"

Dharma studied the faces of Josh and his professor as Josh reflected about his past. She knew the answer and after a few minutes of silence so did Josh.

"I loved becoming my own person," Josh said. "I loved doing my own thing. It made me feel alive. And I also loved the fact that I was always learning and growing. Every day I was becoming more of the person I felt I was supposed to be and could be."

"So there you have it," Mr. Goldman said. "As you think about those answers and how they and college have prepared you to live your purpose, I believe you will find the answers you seek. Becoming more of the person you were born to be is what life is all about.

"In my research about the origin of music, I have come to believe that we are a part of the one song. We exist to create the symphony of life. Each one of us has a note to play, and you can't play anyone else's note. Your job is to play *your* note and contribute to the one song. It's a note you were destined to play from before you were born. And when you discover it and play it with joy to the best of your ability, the creator smiles." Mr. Goldman then stood up, gave Josh a hug, patted Dharma on the head, and said, "I'm glad you came back. While I'm sorry you won't find your purpose here, I hope I offered some something of value to help you find it."

"You did," Josh said. He was thankful for the professor's wisdom, but nonetheless felt sad and mad. He was sad about not playing his note. He knew that for great music to happen each person had to bring his or her skill for playing a particular instrument and specific notes to create a collective sound, and yet right now he felt like a musician on stage who had forgotten the music he was supposed to play. He didn't want to play the note of another. He wanted to play his note, but unfortunately he didn't know what it was. Forget about contributing to the symphony of life. If he were on stage right now he would probably be booed off for producing sounds unpleasant to the human ear.

He was mad at the signs that brought him here. They were supposed to show him the way and guide him in the right direction. But now he felt more hopeless and lost than ever. He walked down the stairs and outside with Dharma and found a bench to sit down on and collect his thoughts. They watched as some students walked to and from class, while others gathered around in front of the building, talking, laughing, and playing. He was envious of them and their happiness. He wanted to be happy again. He knew he could be if he could just find the right place to plant his seed and realize his purpose. He wished he could plant the seed right here. He certainly had been a lot happier in college than he was in his current job.

He thought of the autonomy and freedom he had in college and realized he didn't have the same feeling when he was at work. He didn't feel like he was making it his own. He felt like he worked on an assembly line and, if he never came back, the company could easily replace him. Someone might say, "Did someone remove a piece of furniture from the office?" Another would respond, "No, but

Josh is no longer here." And the original speaker would say, "Oh, I knew *something* was different." Josh felt that he and the furniture left similar impacts.

He stood up from the bench, took a deep breath, and surveyed the area one more time. "If not here, then where? Where else was I happy?" he asked as he gave Dharma a hug and kissed her face. "Where else could I possibly plant this seed?" He looked up to the sky, "If you can give a clear sign, a very clear sign, I really could use one right now."

Chapter 11

Positive Point of View

Dharma knew about signs. Sometimes they came right away. Other times they came when you least expected them. They weren't always clear, and sometimes they made you feel more lost than you were. The important thing was to always look for them and follow them, because they would eventually lead you to the right place.

After Josh asked for a sign, he and Dharma walked across campus to where his car was parked. It was time to leave college and get back on the road. Josh didn't know where they were going, but he knew they were going somewhere.

They walked down a steep hill to his car. As Josh opened the car door to let Dharma in, he noticed a college student getting out of a car parked parallel to his on the other side of the road. The young man maneuvered himself into a wheelchair that was facing up hill.

As Josh walked toward the college student, he realized that the young man was catching his breath and preparing to head up the hill that he and Dharma had just come down. The college student made about three pushes as Josh approached him. Josh asked where he was going, and the student indicated he was headed to the top of the hill, which was quite steep. Josh then asked the young man if he could push him up the hill, and the young man accepted his offer. When Josh took the handles of the wheelchair, it felt unexpectedly light. They climbed steadily up the hill, talking about the love they shared for their college and the beautiful campus—even with all its hills.

When they arrived at the top, the young man said his name was Solomon and that he really appreciated the help. Josh tried not to look at Solomon's legs as he replied, "I'm Josh, and it was my pleasure."

"I usually like to climb the hill myself, but when you offered, I thought, why not? I deserve a break," the young man said with a lighthearted laugh. He looked down, pausing for a moment. "You know, in my dreams I can still run up these hills like I use to when my legs worked," the young man said.

"What happened?" Josh inquired, looking at Solomon's legs for the first time.

"Car accident," he said shaking his head. "It was a freak thing. We had just played in the football state final. I had the game of my life. College recruiters were there. After the game, I was driving with a few friends to a party when we were blindsided by a drunk driver. My best friend died. My other friend suffered only a concussion, and me . . . I was paralyzed from the waist down. In one moment our lives were changed forever."

"I'm sorry," Josh said, not knowing what else to say.

"Don't be sorry for me," Solomon said. "I'm thankful I'm alive. Every day when I think of my friend who died, I decide to live each day to the fullest for him. Hills like this are nothing compared to the mountains I've faced in my life."

"I bet," Josh said, knowing Solomon was wise beyond his years. "So, what brought you to this college?" he asked.

"My grandfather use to be a football coach here. Everyone called him Coach Ken."

"I met him once," Josh said. "He was a legend."

"Yes he was. I used to run around the football field and run up these hills when I visited him with my parents. My dream was to play football here. Then, after my accident, I gave up on the dream. I couldn't see myself here and not playing football. So I applied to a bunch of other schools as well. But one night after talking to my mom, I realized I had more to offer the world than just playing football. She told me that some visions have to die for new ones to be born. So here I am. Climbing hills. Going to class. Waiting for a new vision."

"That makes two of us," Josh thought. He looked at his watch. Dharma was waiting in the car for him.

"Do you have any ideas of what your vision might be?"

"Not sure. I'm thinking I might want to coach or be an entrepreneur and own my own business. Either way, I know I want to be a leader."

Josh smiled. "I can see that, for sure."

"I appreciate the encouragement," Solomon said. "Most people wouldn't say it to my face, but I know they think it will be hard for me to lead from a wheelchair—but those who think that haven't studied history. Franklin Delano Roosevelt was one of the greatest leaders in U.S. history, and he was in a wheelchair. My legs may be weak, but my character and will are strong. I've become a possibility thinker. I don't think about what is impossible. I focus on what is possible." Solomon then looked at his cell phone and realized how the time had passed. "Oh, man, speaking of what's possible, I have to get to class as fast as possible," he quipped. "Big lecture I can't miss. It was great meeting you," he said reaching out his hand. They shook hands, and Josh walked away nodding his head, knowing that Solomon had one thing he needed more of—*hope*. And as Solomon headed off to class to learn and grow, Josh headed back to his car, thinking of new possibilities where he could plant the seed.

As they drove away from campus, Josh couldn't stop thinking and talking about Solomon. He talked to Dharma about how he felt guilty and ashamed for feeling sorry for himself. Solomon was facing a far more difficult situation, and he wasn't complaining. "He isn't the impaired one. I am. The truth is, I have no real problems," he said. "I have no reason to complain. I have my health. I have undiscovered dreams still in my heart and a life of possibilities that await me. I just need to continue the journey to find out where to plant my seed."

Glancing at Dharma, he continued, "You know what, girl? I may never see Solomon again, but in three short blocks and a simple conversation, he gave me a gift that I'll never forget. The way he spoke, his smile, and the hope in his eyes—he gave me a gift."

Josh didn't have to say what it was. Dharma understood. It was the gift of perspective. It was a gift that human beings needed as they faced the ups and downs of life. She understood it was an essential gift, because humans don't live their lives based on reality but rather on their perception of reality.

She called this a person's *point of view* (POV), and it can actually be a gift or a curse, depending on how one uses it to see the world. Dharma observed these gifts and curses playing out every day. When it rains, for example, some humans grumble about getting wet, while others are thankful because their yards and flowers need water.

She also noticed how different people react to different challenges. Some choose to see a positive outcome, while others choose to see a negative outcome. She thought this was interesting since the outcomes were as yet unknown.

Their POVs determine how people feel and act. One person may be filled with positive emotions and energized by a given situation, while another may be paralyzed by fear. Yes, indeed, POV is very important, because how you see the world defines your world. Dharma was glad that Solomon helped Josh see things differently. Solomon helped him turn his POV into what she called a PPOV—*positive point of view*—and Dharma knew that in doing so, Josh would enhance his J-O-Y.

Just as Josh was able to see the maze from a new and higher perspective while in the airplane, he now saw his situation from a completely different point of view. He wasn't lost. He was just somewhere between where he was and where he wanted to go. The great news was that Solomon gave him a sign, a gift, and a clue about where to go next.

Chapter 12

Dogs Have a Purpose

Dharma thought it was amusing that humans thought so much about their purpose. After all, dogs didn't have to think much about it. A dog just knows. A dog just lives it every day. Yes, dogs have a purpose, and it is simply to love people unconditionally. She loved the old joke, "If you want to know who loves you unconditionally, lock your wife, your mother-in-law, and your dog in the trunk of your car. An hour later, open the trunk and notice who is happy to see you." Yes, dogs don't care what you do. They still love you, no matter what.

Humans become confused, Dharma thought, because they have a desire to learn and grow. It's part of their design. They focus so much on the learning and growing that they forget the art of *being*. They focus so much on striving against one another that they forget they were made for loving one another. Humans were made to learn and grow. Dogs were made to just be. But both were made to love unconditionally. From Dharma's point of view, people would be a lot better off if they learned to just be and to focus on loving unconditionally. Humans needed to simplify things and stop making everything so complicated.

If Dharma could talk, she would tell him to simplify and not let what you have to do at work get in the way of what you love to do. She knew that people don't love everything they have to do in the course of their day. It's what makes being a human being much harder than being a dog. The key is to focus on the "one thing" about your job that you love instead of concentrating on all the stuff that drains you. Stress, busyness, deadlines, disagreements, and office politics are powerless in the face of love.

Josh just needed to remember what he loved. Dharma wished she could tell him what it was. But since it wasn't her place to do so, she was thrilled they were headed to a destination that would give him some answers.

Yes, dogs have a purpose, and Dharma's purpose was to love Josh—to love him despite all his faults, mistakes, and humanness. He wasn't perfect. He didn't always do the right thing, and sometimes he made the wrong decisions. He was a work in progress, but she loved him unconditionally.

Chapter 13

The Restaurant

Carroll surveyed the empty dining room. She didn't want to think about how bad business was. Instead, she chose to remember the good old days—when the dining room was always packed, when customers would wait an hour for a table, when the owners put employees and quality and customer service before numbers and profit. Unfortunately, those days were gone. The new owners who had bought the place were so focused on, and skilled at, cutting costs that they also cut their profits along the way. Funny, Carroll thought, how businesses that put profits before people wind up losing the people that provide the profits. She longed for the good old days, and when she looked toward the front door and watched people walk into the restaurant, she was reminded of what the good old days were all about.

Josh walked in and spotted Carroll immediately. She had the same fiery red hair and the same rotund figure that revealed she spent too much time in the restaurant. Despite being only 10 years older than Josh, she was one of the best leaders he had ever met.

"Where is everyone?" he asked. "This used to be your busiest time."

"Don't get me started," Carroll said. "New owners. We won't make it another month."

Josh sighed in disbelief. Another place in which he had planned to plant the seed was about to become non-existent.

"So . . . how are you doing, stranger?" Carroll asked, as she gave Josh a big hug. "It's so good to see you. I miss your enthusiasm around here. I think it's been about five years since you worked here."

"Yep, five years," Josh said. He couldn't believe it had been that long. On one hand, it seemed like yesterday, yet he also felt that a different person had been living his life back then. Had he really followed his college girlfriend to the city where she and her family lived? Had he really waited tables here while pursuing a career in music? Had it really ended so horribly wrong? Perhaps he felt like a different person now because his life had changed so much. Or perhaps the pain of the past made him *wish* he were a different person.

Josh and his college girlfriend had talked often about their dreams and getting married. They had planned to move to a city where neither of their parents lived to start a life together. But then she'd changed her mind. Pressure from her parents had made her return home, and Josh was faced with a choice. He could go with her or let her go. He knew that long-distance relationships weren't for him. He hadn't wanted to move to her hometown, but he'd done it for love. He would do anything for love. When he arrived, he searched for a job in a strange city where he had no money and no family. He had found a job waiting tables at the restaurant where he now stood and had started playing acoustic music at different bars around the city. Although everything seemed to be going okay, he kept getting the feeling that he was supposed to be somewhere else. He begged his girlfriend to leave with him, but she wouldn't go. Either the pull of her family was too strong or her love for Josh was too weak.

The feeling to leave grew stronger, and one day he told his girlfriend that he was going to leave. They both knew what that meant, because she was unwilling to go and he was unwilling to stay. It was the most painful decision of his life, and he drove 11 straight hours to his parents' house with a broken heart and an uncertain future. His only consolation was that he got to keep Dharma.

He left his girlfriend, his job waiting tables, and his music career behind. Eventually, after much soul searching, he pursued a career in business and found a great job in the city where he'd always wanted to live and where he still lived. Although he tried to forget the pain of the past, he always remembered the great experiences he had waiting tables—and it was those memories, and Carroll, that brought him back to the restaurant on this day. She had given him a job when he needed it and had taught him everything he knew about customer service. It was there he had learned the art of interacting with customers and developed the confidence to talk to anyone about anything. Most of all, despite the drawback that it was located in same city where his ex-girlfriend resided, the restaurant was a place where he had been happy.

As Carroll and Josh talked about old times and about his current life, the restaurant unexpectedly started to fill up. A popular movie had just premiered at the theater nearby, and it seemed everyone from the movie was coming to the restaurant at once. Knowing she was desperately understaffed to handle a dinner crowd like this, Carroll grew increasingly nervous. She was trying to think of who she could call to come in at a moment's notice, when Josh volunteered to help out.

"I can't let you do that," she said. "You're big-time now."

"I don't mind," Josh said. "I'd love to help you out. It will do me some good. I just hope I remember everything."

"It's like riding a bike. You never forget. Let's rock and roll!" she said as she grabbed Josh's arm and they ran to help a staff in the weeds.

Carroll was right. Once he started taking orders, helping out in the kitchen, and serving food, it felt like he'd never left; despite his sore feet at the end of the night, Josh felt great. He loved helping out a friend in need, but most of all, he loved the satisfaction of seeing customers enjoy their meals.

That night as he went to bed in a nearby hotel, with Dharma by his side, he felt better about himself than he had in a long time. He decided he would take Carroll up on her offer. She needed help for a few more days while the newly released movie was still popular and asked if he could be her assistant manager, waiter, kitchen help, and anything else she needed until she could hire a few more people. Why not, he thought? He had plenty of time on his hands, a friend in need, and a desire to serve.

Chapter 14

Service

For the next five days Josh did everything he could to help run the restaurant. While Dharma slept in the manager's office, he took orders, served food, cleared off tables, washed dishes, cooked, and greeted customers. Anything Carroll needed him to do he did, but his favorite part was greeting and talking to the customers.

He met all kinds of people with all kinds of personalities. Some treated him with kindness and respect, while others treated him like a servant who was beneath them. They had no idea of his background or that he was responsible for some of the commercials they saw on television. To some, he was simply a waiter, someone with nothing better to do with his life. For this reason, Josh thought everyone should have to wait tables at some point in their life. They would have a new appreciation for the restaurant business and the people who serve. They would understand that those who serve are real people with real, families, real challenges, hopes, and dreams. Once people experienced life as a waiter, they would never again be rude to servers, and they would give bigger tips, too.

In his role as a waiter, Josh knew it didn't matter what people thought about him. What mattered was how he felt about serving. He loved it! The minute he started serving others, all his problems went away. Instead of worrying about his life, his future, and his job, he was focused on making sure other people were happy. He wasn't sure whether he was the only one who felt this way about serving, but when he met Pamela, a coworker, he knew he wasn't alone. As much as Josh loved serving, Pamela seemed to love it more. One day while on a break, Josh asked her why she loved her job so much. "It's the people," she said. "I just love the customers."

"Even the negative ones?" Josh asked, always trying to learn something from everyone he met. He was a student of life, and he wanted to know what made Pamela tick.

"Yes, even the negative ones," she said, smiling. "But I don't see them as negative. I see them as people who need more love and attention. I think they are negative because they've been let down before. They've had bad service and have lost their faith in people. I see it as my job to earn their trust. To show them I am willing to do whatever it takes to make their meal enjoyable. And it's so funny. The more I love them and earn their trust, the more they open up to me, and their negativity melts away. It takes a little more effort, but it's so much more meaningful."

"Do they appreciate it?" Josh asked.

"Oh, yes," Pamela said. "I've been working here for four years, and I have a wall full of holiday cards at my house from so many of my customers. They come in with their families, and I've been able to watch their children grow. Even when the place is slow, which has been a lot lately, my section is always full because so many people ask for me."

After meeting Pamela, Josh realized why he loved waiting tables so much. Like Pamela, he loved to serve.

Josh also noticed something else about working at the restaurant. Despite working harder and expending more physical energy at the restaurant than at his "real" job, he felt more energized at the end of the day. The more energy he shared with a service mind-set, the more he was refueled. He decided that hard work doesn't make you tired. A bad attitude is what makes you tired.

Josh thought of these things as he waited outside the restaurant to say good-bye to Carroll. He had worked there for five days, the movie was no longer popular, the restaurant had slowed down considerably, and Josh knew it was time for him to leave and figure out where to go next.

Carroll met Josh and Dharma outside to say good-bye and to ask him one more time to stay and work at the restaurant with her until they could open their own restaurant together. But Josh knew that although the restaurant reminded him of his desire to serve, he wasn't meant to be in the restaurant business. He was meant to apply what he loved about waiting tables to his current job or a new one. He was meant to bring a server's mind-set to whatever career he chose.

Chapter 15

Gifts from the Past

Looking at the restaurant one last time as he drove away, Josh came to the realization that wherever he decided to plant the seed, it wouldn't be at a place from his past. While the signs pointed him to the places where he had been happy, he wasn't meant to plant the seed there—he realized he was meant to rediscover what energized him and brought him happiness in his past.

He remembered what the pilot had told him and saw how his past had provided him with clues for his future. Going home reminded him of his strengths and gifts. At college he discovered he loved learning, growing, and being autonomous. At the restaurant he rediscovered his passion for serving others.

Unfortunately, he wasn't doing any of these things at his current job. He wasn't making his work his own. He wasn't learning and growing like he did in college and wasn't serving others like he did at the restaurant. He felt stagnant, and he wasn't sure whether it was his company's fault or his own. What he was sure of was that whether he stayed in his current job or found a new job, he needed to make some changes.

From now on he would use his strengths to learn, to grow, and to serve. Instead of feeling like he was dying every day, he would start living. He wasn't supposed to be a pastor. He wasn't supposed to be a teacher or professor. And he wasn't meant to be in the restaurant business. He was supposed to take the elements of what he loved about these past experiences and make them a part of his life, with the hope that they would lead him to his purpose. He just hoped he would find his purpose within the next week—before he had to give his boss a decision.

Chapter 16

A New Opportunity

As Josh drove along the highway listening to "Don't Stop Believing," by Journey, he wasn't sure where he was headed next. It was a strange feeling to drive without a destination in mind, but lately he had come to embrace the adventure of uncertainty. He was visiting old places and rediscovering new things about himself. It was uncomfortable not knowing what tomorrow would bring, and yet he felt a surprising sense of peace that he was on the right path. He believed if he waited for a sign and expected one, it would come. And as he was walking out of the bathroom at a gas station, a sign did come—in the form of a call on his cell phone, a call that would give him a new direction on his journey.

It was a headhunter he had met at an industry conference in Las Vegas six months earlier. She had asked him for his card and told him she helped companies find and hire talented people like him. He gave her his card, never expecting to get a call, and yet here she was, of all times, telling him she had an opportunity for him. They spoke for about 10 minutes, and when the call ended, Josh told Dharma what she had said.

"Can you believe it, girl? She told me I was a rising star in the profession and a lot of companies know about me. She said she has a company that wants to meet with me tomorrow. They are located in a different city, and I'd have to fly there, but they want to hire me, so the interview is just a formality. This could be the answer to our prayers. This is it. I bet I'm supposed to plant the seed at this new job. The timing couldn't be more perfect."

Dharma hadn't seen him this excited in a long time and as they made the long trek back to his apartment, Josh became quiet as he fantasized about what his new job would be like.

Josh imagined himself in a new city and a new building, working in a different office with renewed passion and energy. He saw himself making his mark on the company with new, fresh ideas. He felt energized with the prospect of learning from new people and growing in a new company. He was ready to bring a service-focused mind-set to his work, and a new job would be a great place to start.

The farmer had been right. He sought his purpose because there was a purpose to be found. But it wasn't meant to be found in the past. He was meant to find it in the future, at his new job, where he could be all he was meant to be. This is where he would plant the seed and live his purpose. It would be a fresh start and an opportunity to grow to new heights.

His excitement and fantasies made the trip seem shorter than it was. They arrived home just before midnight, and Josh immediately gathered his things and prepared for an early-morning flight. His neighbor would look after Dharma for the day, and he would take the first flight home after his interview and arrive late in the evening. The only thing left to do was to get a good night's sleep so he could be at the top of his game.

The next morning his alarm clock shook him out of a deep sleep. He had wanted to wake up feeling fresh, but he felt like he needed eight more hours of sleep. He'd had the same dream again about planting the seed on his desk and then moving the plant to a large field. The meaning of the dream was still unclear, but he figured it was a sign that he was on the right path.

After a quick breakfast of Grape-Nuts, and a banana, Josh gave Dharma a hug, raced to the airport, and ran through the terminal to make it to his gate on time. While waiting in line to board the plane, he looked outside the window and saw a bunch of dark clouds overhead. Thunderstorms were moving into the area, and he hoped they wouldn't delay his flight. He had only a short window of time between his plane's scheduled landing and his interview. Any delay could mess up his plans.

When the gate agent scanned his ticket into the computer before he boarded the plane, she gave him great news. He had been upgraded to first class! Another sign that encouraged Josh to think that his future was bright.

He arrived at his seat, gave the flight attendant his suit jacket, and decided he was going to smile at everyone who walked by him. It was fun to see who would smile back, who would think he was crazy, and who would totally ignore him.

He also observed the flight attendants and could tell which ones loved their job, which ones were indifferent, and which ones not only hated their job but hated every passenger on board. It was interesting, he thought, that different people could do the same exact job and approach it in completely different ways. He took note of one flight attendant who smiled sincerely at the passengers and also made people laugh during the announcements. She wasn't just collecting a paycheck, she was making a difference. Like Pamela from the restaurant, she stood out among the people she worked with. Unfortunately, another flight attendant also stood out, but it was because of her nasty demeanor. Was she so miserable because she was having a bad day or because she was burned out?

It occurred to Josh that it's not the job you do that matters. It's the energy and mind-set that you bring to your job that truly matters. He thought that burnout is more often caused by purpose deficiency than vitamin deficiency, and it was something from which he was definitely suffering. He took plenty of vitamins, yet he still felt tired at work. He wasn't standing out like the flight attendant who was making a difference. He had become another brick in the wall. Working with passion and purpose was something he was looking forward to doing at his new job—if the plane would ever take off.

The pilot made an announcement over the loudspeaker that thunderstorms were moving in and that they were going to try to take off quickly to beat the storms.

"That would be great," Josh said out loud as he looked around to check out the other passengers in first class. He thought it was both crazy and sad that some people could be sitting next to someone for a few hours on a plane and not say a single word to that person. Not even "Hello," "How are you," or "Hi, my name is so-and-so; please don't talk to me so I can take a nap." He believed in at least introducing himself to everyone he sat next to on a plane, and, as a result, he had met some amazing people and had some interesting conversations. His secret was the five-minute rule. He would introduce himself and talk to the person next to him for five minutes. If there was a connection, if they were meant to share and learn from one another, he would know it within five minutes and then talk to the person for the rest of the flight. If there wasn't a connection, he would pull out his iPad and listen to music, watch a movie, read a book, or do some work.

As Josh prepared to introduce himself to the middle-aged man next to him, who looked like a 55-year-old executive for a Fortune 500 company, he wondered whether the conversation would last longer than five minutes.

Chapter 17

George

The man next to him was reading his newspaper when Josh turned toward him to introduce himself.

"Hello, my name is Josh."

The man glanced up from his paper, put it aside, faced Josh, and shook his hand. "I'm George. Nice to meet you."

"Hope the flight takes off on time."

"Me too," said George, willingly engaging in Josh's small talk. "Do you have an important meeting to get to?"

"I do. For a job interview."

"Oh," George said, nodding his head. "Have you been looking for a job for a long time?"

Josh laughed. "Actually no, I already have a job. This is a different company that wants to hire me. It's a long story, but I've been on a two-week vacation, and out of blue I got this call from a headhunter about a great new opportunity, so here I am. I wasn't looking for it. It came to me."

"So, you're unhappy in your job?" George asked.

"No, I'm not unhappy," Josh answered. "I just think I might be happier in this new job. It seems like a great opportunity."

"What makes you think you might be happier there?"

"I don't know," Josh said, shaking his head. "I just have a feeling, I guess."

George shook his head and laughed, but not because he was amused. Josh knew he was laughing for a different reason. Josh looked at his watch. The conversation had lasted two minutes, and it was time to pull out his iPad.

But George continued before Josh could grab it, "I'm sorry for laughing," George said sincerely. "It's just that everyone always thinks they'll be happier somewhere else. They move from job to job, marriage to marriage, looking for something more, when the place they should be looking is within themselves. The old saying is true, 'Wherever you go, there you are.' When you get to be my age, you realize it's not about your boss. It not about finding a new job to make you happier. It's about you. Our happiness has less to do with forces outside of us and more to do with what's inside of us. Happiness is an inside job. It's a choice."

"But don't you think certain jobs will make you happier than others?" Josh asked. "For instance, I think I'd be miserable if I had to deal with numbers all day like an accountant."

George, put his hand on his chin and thought for a moment. "Of course, there are certain jobs that will energize you more than others. Some people love numbers, so they'd love a job that deals with them. If you love a job and are good at it, there is a greater probability that you'll be happier doing it. However, there's more to the story when it comes to being happy at work.

"I've met bus drivers, janitors, and fast-food employees who are more passionate about their jobs and happier than executives making millions of dollars. I'm convinced that our happiness comes not from the work we do, but from how we feel about the work we do.

"The way we think about work, feel about work, and approach our work influences our happiness at work." Then George paused for a moment and in a soft voice said, "Josh, I believe you'll be happy wherever you decide to be happy."

At that moment, the pilot made another announcement that didn't make Josh very happy: Air traffic control had put a hold on all flights leaving the airport. They could taxi back to the gate and let the passengers off, but then it would take a lot more time to reload the passengers in the event the plane received clearance for takeoff; the better option would be to remain on the plane so that when the skies cleared they could take off immediately. The delay was expected to be an hour.

Josh asked George to excuse him for a moment as he turned on his cell phone, called the headhunter, and left a message that his plane had been delayed, that he would not be able to make it on time for the interview, and that hopefully they could reschedule later in the day.

"If it's meant to happen it will happen," George said reassuringly to Josh, who at that moment wasn't feeling so confident. "Someone told me once that everything happens for a reason, and I've come to live my life by that."

But Josh wasn't listening. He was thinking about what George had said about happiness, and he remembered what the farmer had said about not letting your mind play tricks on you and about following your heart. Was he following his mind instead of his heart? Was his focus on happiness misleading him? He was more confused than ever.

"How do you know this new opportunity isn't right for me?" Josh asked. "Who's to say that it's not God's plan for me to take this new job?"

George laughed, but this time it was because he was amused. "I can't pretend to know God's plan. Only God is God. But I do know that you just have to be careful when you make happiness your GPS system in life." Confirming Josh's thoughts, he added, "Happiness can be deceiving, elusive, and misleading. I've had a few friends who have opened restaurants because they love to cook only to find they were miserable because of all the stuff that came with it. I have another friend who loves to paint, but she wouldn't want to do it for a living. And my wife's best friend is happiest when she is decorating, but she was unhappy working as an interior decorator. The fact is, just because you are happy doing something doesn't mean that you should make it your life's work. Some hobbies are meant to be hobbies, not careers."

Josh knew this to be true. He felt the same way about the ministry. He was sure it wasn't his calling. But what he wasn't sure of now was whether he should join a new company just because he thought he would be happier there. Maybe he was wrong to pursue happiness?

A few seconds later he received a call from the headhunter. Rescheduling the interview wasn't a problem. She told Josh to give her a call when the plane was about to take off and the company would work around his schedule. The news made Josh much more relaxed. A sign, he thought, that George was wrong. He would be happier at the new job.

"Well, if I shouldn't use happiness as my guidance system, what *should* I use? How do I know whether I should take a new job or stay in the one I have?" he asked.

George thought for minute. He had spent a lifetime thinking about such questions and, knowing not everyone believed what he believed, wanted to explain his answer in a way Josh would understand.

"First, I would say that you should look for the signs and follow them."

For the first time all morning, Josh was excited. "So, you believe in signs, too?" George was relieved. Without Josh's belief in signs, the conversation probably would have ended right then. "Yes, I believe in signs," George replied, his eyes lighting up, "ever since I met a bus driver who showed me how to look beyond road signs and to follow the signs that guide you through life."

"But what happens when the signs aren't clear?" asked Josh. Sometimes they seem to be pointing in both directions, if you know what I mean."

"I know what you mean," George said. "When the signs aren't clear, you ask a few simple questions: *Have I learned all that I'm meant to learn in my current job? Is there still an opportunity for me to grow there? Have I put my heart and soul into my work to be the best that I can be? Have I reached my full potential?*"

"If you've learned all you can learn at your job and there's no room to grow and you've given everything you have to your work there and you feel as though you've reached your full potential, then it's time to move on. However, if there is still something for you to learn where you are and there is still an opportunity for you to grow and you haven't reached your full potential there, then you are meant to stay. You stay and you decide to devote 100 percent of your energy to being the best you can be."

"If you are meant to develop yourself somewhere else, something will happen to remove you from your job. You'll either get a promotion in the form of a new position with your company or you'll get a promotion in the form of being fired, which is a sign that there's a better job out there for you. People experience job losses all the time, and when that happens I know it's because they are meant to learn and grow somewhere else. They see it as being fired. I see it as a promotion. I've learned that adversity is not a dead end but a detour to a better outcome than you can imagine. Can I tell you a story that might make things more clear?"

Josh looked at his watch. They were well past the hour's delay and the sky outside was still as black as night.

He knew they had nothing but time, and he still had things to learn. "Sure," said Josh, hoping George's story would help him make his decision easier.

"Years ago, I got on this bus to go to work—not by choice, mind you, but because my car was broken down. My marriage, my job, and my life were falling apart. I didn't want to talk to anybody. But the driver of the bus wouldn't let me sit there drowning in my sorrows. We started talking, and she changed the course of my life. Ever since, I made a pact that I'll talk to anyone I can help and who could possibly help me. I've learned we are all teachers and students, and a life touches a life that touches a life.

"So, after this bus driver helps me, my career starts to take off. I go from being a marketing manager to being a director of marketing, and eventually I was running an entire region for my company. Work was great. My family was happy. I was happy. Then one day a recruiter calls and asks me if I would consider working for other companies. I don't know why I said yes, but I did. Next thing you know, I start getting all these offers, and my mind, the great deceiver, starts telling me I'd be even happier elsewhere; I can have more power and influence at a new company, and I can make even more money for my family. So I get an offer and decide to leave. But looking back, I hadn't reached my full potential where I was. I still had room to grow. I left too soon. Looking back, the signs were very clear, but I ignored them out of pride.

"Well, I join this new company and within a year the economy starts to tank and I get laid off. Now I'm lost.

'Who's going to hire a guy in his fifties?' I ask. One day I'm walking on the beach where we have a summer house that's about to be foreclosed on and I think life would be a lot easier if I just jump into the ocean. But then I thought of my son, who at the time was probably just a little younger than you, and I thought, 'If I give up now, what lesson am I teaching my son? If I don't overcome my challenges, my son will learn to let his challenges overcome him. I need to show my son that even though Dad was knocked down, he can get back up . . . so when life knocks him down he'll know that he can get back up, too.'

"I was inspired with a bigger purpose after that to show my son that I could get back up after being knocked down. I dusted off my resume, called friends and colleagues in the industry, and reached out to various companies, letting them know I was back in the game. During the next few months, I had a bunch of interviews and received several offers, and now I'm doing my best every day to improve and grow at my new company. Interestingly enough, I'm in the same position I held in my old company, running a region."

"Wow, what an amazing story," Josh said, thinking of how his own dad had inspired him throughout his life. "I bet your son is really proud of you."

"He is," said George. "And so are my wife and daughter. One thing I know is that the greatest lesson we can share with our children is the way we live our life and how we respond to adversity. Getting fired was the hardest thing I ever had to go through, but looking back, I realize the job loss was a lesson I had to learn for having left my job when I wasn't ready. These days, every young gun wants to be CEO but doesn't want to go through the process of preparation. I've learned you can't rush it. It's not about where you will be happier. The future usually seems more appealing than the present because it's more about fantasy than reality. The key is to make your fantasy your reality where you are. This goes for work, relationships, and life."

Josh looked at his phone and read the text he had received from the headhunter. She was wondering if there were any updates. Josh texted back, "Still delayed. Waiting for an answer." He was waiting for an answer from the pilot, but he was also waiting for an answer about what he should do. George made a lot of sense, yet the temptation of a new job was too powerful to ignore. He looked up at George, who continued to make his case "So, in making your decision, don't choose where you will be happiest—choose where you will learn the most. Choose where you can grow into your full potential. If you've grown all you can grow where you are and it's time to grow higher somewhere else, then leave. But don't leave because of challenges. Where you experience resistance, you find the lessons that you are meant to learn. People often run when they face resistance, but to grow you must face it and learn from it. We often have to go through things at work and in life that don't make us happy, but they teach us lessons that lead to our happiness in the future. Every job, good or bad, trains us for the work we are meant to do in the future. Challenges only make you stronger."

Josh nodded, knowing George was right. Perhaps he was running from his challenges. Maybe he was running to a fantasy instead of creating a meaningful reality. "What should I do?" Josh asked with desperation in his voice as he looked at the texts on his phone.

"Decide to put your heart and soul into your work," George said with conviction. "I stopped doing this, and it was one of the reasons I left. But looking back, it wasn't the job that changed, it was me. I now know that if you bring your passion to work and are purposeful about what you are doing, happiness will be a by-product. You won't have to search for it. Happiness will find you."

Josh couldn't believe George had just mentioned *passion* and *purpose*. If he was ever looking for a sign, this one was it. He felt the seed in his pocket and remembered what the farmer had said. Find out where to plant it and your purpose will be revealed to you. He was in such deep thought that he almost didn't hear the pilot announce that they were heading back to the gate. The flight had been canceled, and the passengers would have to rebook on another flight.

Josh walked off the plane feeling tired, frustrated, and conflicted. He said good-bye to George, exchanged business cards with him, and thanked him for his advice. George was someone he definitely wanted to keep in touch with. He looked at the large airport monitor for additional flights to his interview city. There were three other flights that could potentially get him there in time for an afternoon meeting. "Should I go?" he asked himself, leaning toward a decision but not fully convinced. "Some obstacles are meant to test us," he thought. "Other obstacles are meant to prevent us from doing something that will harm us. Which one was this?"

He remembered the farmer telling him to listen to his heart; thus he decided to follow the signs that resonated most with it and spoke the loudest to it. George had spoken the truth he needed to hear; Josh believed that George's words and the canceled flight were signs meant to put him on the right path. He turned away from the monitor, walked toward the airport exit, and called the headhunter. He wouldn't be taking the next flight. He wouldn't be going to the interview. He was going back to work to reach his full potential.

Chapter 18

The Decision

It's easy to decide to do something. The hard part is actually doing it. Josh thought about this as he drove home from the airport. George had talked about happiness being a by-product of working with passion and purpose. The question now was, could he actually do this in his current job? Could he learn, grow, and serve in a job that had become stale. The idea of a new job at a different company had been an exciting fantasy, and now he hoped he could turn that fantasy into a reality at his current job.

He looked at the seed in his hand. "Yes, I know where to plant it now," he told himself. When George had talked about growing to his full potential, his heart knew before he did. You can't plant your seed in the past, and you can't plant it in the future. The only place you can plant it is in your present.

The answer had been right in front of him, but he hadn't seen it. He should have known. The answers to life's greatest questions are always the simplest. He would plant his seed at the job he was in now. He would put his heart and soul into his work and bring his love of learning, growing, and serving with him.

As George had said, if he was meant to grow at his company, he would. And if he was meant to be promoted and replanted somewhere else, it would happen. His job was to trust the process and plant his seed in the present opportunity—wherever it was.

He remembered that the farmer had told him to come back when he found where to plant the seed. Because he had a few days left until he needed to give his boss a decision, Josh decided to go back to see the farmer the next day. He had decided where to plant his seed, yet his purpose hadn't been revealed to him. Perhaps the farmer would help him see what he was missing.

Chapter 19
GPT

When Josh walked into his apartment, he saw Dharma lying on the floor. She looked up at him with an expression that said, "I've been waiting for you."

She rolled over on her back as Josh dove to the floor to rub her belly. "If you want to know what pure joy is all about it, it's right here," she wanted to tell him. But he didn't know what pure joy was because he was always rushing the future. Like most humans, he wanted the future to happen *now*, but he was unable to enjoy the now.

"It's a sad condition," thought Dharma, "that affects far too many people, including Josh. Humans spend so much of their time living in the past and imagining the future that they don't fully enjoy the moment." Dogs knew how to enjoy the moment. But for humans, it was one of their biggest challenges. Dogs were limited by the inability to speak, but humans were limited by their busy minds.

She also noticed that younger people like Josh had a more severe condition of rushing the future. It seemed as though the younger people were, the more they thought the universe revolved around them and their timing. She often heard Josh's friends talk about being president of their companies by the time they were 30. She wanted to tell Josh and his friends that the universe doesn't run on their time. It runs on *God's perfect timing* (GPT). There is a time and a season for everything. There is a time for action and a time for rest. There is a time for events to happen and a time for delays. Delays in life happen for a reason. Humans don't like delays, but they are essential for a human's preparation and growth. During delays you reflect, learn, improve, and allow people, circumstances, and events to line up, and in God's perfect timing, everything happens the way it's intended. There is a process that you are meant to go through in order to be shaped and prepared for your future and delays and challenges are part of this process. It's a process you can't rush. Rushing only creates stress that prevents you from seeing and following the signs that will lead you on the right path. Rushing causes you to take on opportunities that you are not prepared for, ultimately leading to failure. The better way is to slow down, follow the process and let life shape you. This prepares you for the future and allows you to enjoy the present.

Dharma didn't know why or how she knew these things. For some reason dogs know things that humans don't. Dogs know things that humans have to figure things out for themselves.

Josh told Dharma that they were going to see the farmer. She was glad because the farmer would teach Josh what she couldn't.

Chapter 20

The Purpose Process

It had been two weeks since Josh and Dharma had visited the farm, yet it felt like a lifetime ago. A strong wind was blowing as the cold air moved in from the north. It was a weekday, so the crowds were gone, and so were the pilot and the line of people waiting to see the maze from a higher perspective. The blue skies had turned gray, and the buzz and excitement that had filled the air two weeks ago was replaced by a quiet stillness. Yes, there is a time for everything, Dharma thought, as Josh left her in the car and went to find the farmer. He searched all around the farm but couldn't find him. He must be in the maze, Josh thought, since there were still some people, mostly parents with young children, making their way through it. Most people were at work or school, but the maze still offered adventure for the young and the young at heart.

He looked at the maze differently now as he approached it. He saw it from a higher perspective and was no longer fearful of getting lost. He entered with the confidence of someone who knew that the beginning and end were connected, and he ran through the maze without fear, looking for the farmer. At one point, he faced a wall of cornstalks and was faced with a choice. Should he go left or right? It reminded him that he had new questions and trusted that the farmer would once again be able to guide him. When he bent down to tie his shoes, he saw the shoes of someone standing in front of him. When he stood up he was glad to see it was the farmer. "I've been looking for you," Josh said with excitement.

"I'm glad you came back, Josh," the farmer said, letting him know he remembered him. "You don't look so lost this time. I suspect your journey has been successful, yes?"

"Well, yes and no," Josh said. "I decided where to plant the seed you gave me, but you said when I found where to plant the seed my purpose would be revealed to me, and it still hasn't revealed itself."

The farmer smiled. "You are right, Josh. I did say it would be revealed to you, but I didn't say it would all happen immediately. It takes time for your purpose to unfold. Even though you want it to happen in two weeks, two days, or two months, it unfolds in its own time. But I can guarantee one thing. I would bet the farm that part of your purpose has been revealed to you. You just don't see it. Let me ask you a question. As you have searched where to plant the seed, what have you learned?"

"I've learned that I need to learn from the past and that the past has prepared me for my future. I've learned that even though I can learn from the past, I can't plant my seed there. I also realize I can't plant my seed in the future. I can only plant my seed where I am, in the present, and so I need to plant my seed at my current job; it is there that I will focus on learning, growing, and serving."

"I told you so," the farmer said. "Your purpose has been revealed to you. Not all of it, but the first layer. You see, purpose is like an onion. It has many layers. The first layer of your purpose is to plant the seed where you are and make the decision to be all that you were created to be—to use your strengths, gifts, and talents to the best of your ability in the service of something bigger than you.

"Once you make this decision to plant the seed where you are, you realize that *you are the seed*, Josh. It's not just about planting the seed. It's about planting *you*. There is a process that seeds must go through in order to become all they are destined to become, and you must go through this same process.

"And as you go through this process, just as the layers of onion peel away, your layers of purpose unfold, and you realize everything in life prepares you to live the purpose for which you were created. It doesn't matter what job you have or whether you are a businessperson, a student, a teacher, or an athlete. It's about planting yourself where you are and becoming a conduit for your bigger purpose to flow through you."

"Well, how long does this process take?" Josh asked, knowing he wanted to live his bigger purpose and yet wondering if he had the patience to go through it.

"It's a process that lasts a lifetime, Josh. Living your purpose is not a one-time event. It *is* the event. Then the farmer paused, picked up a stalk of corn, looked at it, and continued, "Now, with that said, different people find their purposes at different times. Some decide to plant themselves when they are younger and others make this decision when they are older. Unfortunately, some never plant themselves, and they live a meaningless existence.

"Everyone is unique and must go through their own unique process and circumstances to find and live their calling. However, one thing is certain: Everyone will go through four stages as their purpose unfolds in their life. The stages unfold at different times for each person, and the duration of each stage depends on each person's unique purpose and journey. But the one constant is that everyone must go through four stages to find and live their purpose. The process doesn't care what age you are or what your vocation is or what school you went to. Its only concern is for your growth into the person you are meant to be."

In that moment, Josh heard wind chimes creating beautiful sounds, and he remembered what his professor said about the music of spheres and playing your note to contribute to the symphony of life. There was indeed a process to creating music—including powerful moments of inspiration and creative flow balanced with times of struggle and doubts. It was exciting, but often challenging, to give birth to a new piece of music, yet it was a process he had gone through many times. It was painful but necessary. Josh had a feeling that the purpose process was the same. The foreboding of pain made him hesitant to go through it, but he knew he had to do it. With reluctance, he asked the farmer to explain the four stages.

Chapter 21

Four Stages of Purpose

The farmer had never told Josh his name, but for some reason Josh felt as though he had known him all his life. His gray hair, mustache, and clothes made him appear old, but as Josh looked closely at his face for the first time, he noticed that it shined with a youthful radiance, and his blue eyes lit up when he talked about purpose.

"You have already been through the first stage," the farmer said. "It is a stage that lasts until a person decides to plant his or her seed. It is the stage of preparation. The *preparation stage* includes your birth, the family you were born into, your weaknesses and strengths, gifts, passions, the place you were born, and the experiences, challenges, and the lessons you have learned throughout your life that prepare you to be planted.

"It is this stage that makes you unique and provides you with the characteristics that determine what you will grow into and become. During this stage, you will likely experience adversity of some kind that prepares you for your calling. Just as you can't know what light is without experiencing the darkness, how can you know the joy of living your purpose without the experience of struggling to find it?"

The farmer then reached down and grabbed some dirt and cupped it in the palm of his hand and showed it to Josh. "Adversity, for many, features a time of drought," he added. "Drought might include a time when ideas, money, good fortune, contacts, and success dry up. It might include a job loss or the death of a loved one or a personal illness. It might include a time of great uncertainty and fear. During such times, you feel like you are in a desert, isolated from the prosperity, health, and success of the world—thirsty and hungry for something to sustain you but hopeless and despairing because you are stuck in the sand and wondering how you are going to get through this.

"However, when you progress to the other stages of purpose and look back at the preparation stage of your life, you'll realize it was the drought that made you the person you are today; your greatest challenge likely served as the preparation to help you live and share your greatest purpose; and the worst event of your life prepared you for the greatest assignment of your life.

"Just as the roots of a plant in an arid climate dig down deeper in search of water, your personal drought causes you to search for answers and a source of strength. And it is this struggle and searching that creates a willingness within you to be planted."

"I couldn't agree more," Josh said. "During the past year, everything dried up. My ideas, passion, success—it all came to a halt. I know it wasn't a severe drought, but the last year has definitely been dry."

"Droughts are droughts. Some are less severe and shorter in duration than others, but they all lead you to a different place. Where did your drought lead you?" the farmer asked.

"It led me to you," Josh answered with conviction. "It led me to search for my purpose. It led me to my past and the decision to plant the seed at my current job."

"And by planting yourself in your job, where do you hope it will lead?" the farmer asked.

"Honestly, I'm hoping it will lead me to feel more passionate and purposeful about work," Josh said, recalling his conversation with George. "And if my bigger purpose can find me as a result, then that would be the ultimate gift."

"I'm glad you said that, because you are about to enter the second stage of purpose, which is the *planting stage*," the farmer said as his face and blue eyes lit up. "The preparation stage prepares you for the planting stage. It helps you find the right place to plant. It prepares you to be planted, and it often presents a defining moment that prompts you to decide where to be planted. Did you have a defining moment?" the farmer asked.

"I did. I met a man on an airplane who told me a story about his life, and I knew it was a sign to guide me in my life."

"Yes, I love the way signs have a way of connecting people on their journeys and providing direction for both. For you, the defining moment was a conversation. For others, it might be a crisis, an illness, a moment of prayer, advice from a friend or stranger, a positive feeling, a conviction in your heart, or a sign that lets every cell in your body know what you are supposed to do. Regardless of what the defining moment is, it is a moment when you decide to plant yourself where you are.

"During the planting stage, you realize it's not about what others want you to be. It's not even about what you want yourself to be. It's about what you were created to be. You see, Josh, the seed must surrender its own vision and desires as it is placed in the ground. It must die to itself so it can give life to something greater—something that will rise up from the ground and grow beyond its humble origin. Whether you work for a company, a hospital, or a school, whether you're an entrepreneur, an athlete, an artist, a singer, or a stay-at-home parent, whatever role you have in life, you decide to plant yourself where you are and you decide to become all you can be in the service of others. Once you plant yourself, then you proceed to the next stage, which has yet to play out for you. It will be an exciting and challenging journey for you, but through all the ups and downs I want you to remember it's all part of the third stage of purpose, which is the *growth stage*."

"How long does the growth stage last?" Josh asked.

"It depends on each person. I can't tell you for sure. Only the designer of the seed and the seed know what it is meant to become and how long it will take to grow and how high it will reach.

"But I can tell you that when you decide to plant yourself, you will begin to grow almost immediately. In this stage, the seed gives birth to the plant. This is where you grow and your roots spread. You will experience all the right conditions to ensure your growth. Beginner's luck happens here. The right people show up and the right situations present themselves in order for you to grow. When you surrender and decide to plant yourself, God will move heaven and earth to ensure your growth so that you will be able to experience the final and fourth stage."

"But growth isn't always easy," Josh said. He had heard enough of his dad's sermons to know that growth is a by-product of both uplifting and challenging experiences.

"Indeed," the farmer said. "You are certainly a wise young man. During the growth process, you will experience events that help you soar to new heights, but you will also face adversity and challenges that strengthen your roots. You will experience nourishment that helps you grow in order to reach the final stage. And you will be pruned like a bush and experience things that appear to be setbacks but are really designed to help you fully grow into all you are meant to become. You will experience moments when you say, 'I can do this' and 'I'm on the right path,' and you will also experience challenges and face people who test your will and make you doubt yourself and your path."

"I understand the challenges you are talking about," Josh said. "My father always said that people often think blessings come in the form of nicely wrapped perfect square boxes, but often they come disguised as wrecking balls meant to crumble the world you know so you can rebuild your life with a new foundation of faith and trust. Sometimes we have to be knocked down so we can grow to greater heights."

"Indeed," said the farmer. "And you can't grow to greater heights without the right foundation."

"I know I'll experience naysayers," Josh said knowing that naysayers often chipped away at his foundation. "They are everywhere at work."

"They are everywhere in life," the farmer responded. "Remember, your purpose and faith must be greater than the opinions of others. You will also face the naysayer within. The critic inside you is far more dangerous and adept at crushing your dreams than anyone else: 'Who am I to be leading others? Who am I to be doing this work. Who am I to be in this position of influence you might ask yourself?' And during these times, your passion and desire to make a difference must overcome your fear and self-doubt. Also remember that God's thoughts are greater than your thoughts and God's plan for your life is greater than your plans. Trust more in God's plan than your own limited thinking and you'll accomplish more than you ever thought possible. You don't have to be great to make a difference. You just have to serve with great desire, and if you do, God will help you overcome your doubts, bless you and bless through you so you can be a blessing to others."

Josh reached down and picked up some dirt and felt the cold earth in his hand. He knew about self-doubt.

Although he was confident in many ways, he had also experienced a lot of self-doubt throughout his life. "I'll also face envy," Josh said, knowing that self-doubt had often reared its ugly head when he compared his success to that of others. Whenever he didn't think he measured up, he tended to become disappointed and disengaged.

"Never, never, never compare yourself to others," countered the farmer. "The great enemy of growth is the belief that you don't matter and that your growth doesn't matter. Just because someone has achieved more material success and reached a higher status doesn't mean they are more important than you. Everyone is on their own path. Everyone's timeline is different. Each person has his or her own purpose and reason for existing. When you focus on your growth and reach the final stage, you'll understand how important you are to the world."

Josh remembered what his professor said about playing your own note, and he was struck by how everything in life works according to the same principles. Music, seeds, and human beings all have a rhythm and a process whereby the part contributes to the whole—a plant contributes to the ecosystem, a note to the symphony, a person to society. Everything does matter he thought. We all matter.

"Well, if I'm important to the world, then I'll surely face obstacles," Josh said, remembering all the stories his dad had shared through the years of overcomers who changed history and the world.

"Indeed," said the farmer, "and it is these obstacles that will test you before you can enter the final stage. We live in a universe of duality: light and dark, up and down, hot and cold. All are part of the whole. As you strive to find your purpose, you'll also encounter the resistance that keeps you from it—and the closer you get to realizing your ultimate purpose, the stronger the resistance becomes. Those who navigate the darkness to find their light reach the final stage. Unfortunately, far too many people give up in the growth stage. The tests become too powerful and overwhelming, and their will and faith falter. Sadly enough, many give up just as they are about to move to the fourth and final stage. If they had persevered throughout, they would have been able to experience the greatest feeling in the world."

"What is the final stage?" Josh asked, desperately wanting to know and experience the greatest feeling in the world.

"I can't tell you," the farmer answered. "It is more powerful when you figure it out for yourself. But I can tell you that as you move from the third to the final stage, your vision and bigger purpose for your life becomes very clear. You may have a sense of this vision during the planting stage, and you may clarify it during the growth stage, but as you reach the final stage, you can articulate it in a sentence with extreme confidence.

"Once you know your purpose you tap into the power that fuels all of creation. You know your reason for being alive, and knowing and living this reason gives you the greatest feeling in the world." With those words, the farmer walked toward the right-hand path and said, "I have another lost person I have to go help. But before I leave I want you to know that God has big plans for you. Don't give up. You are very important to the world. Don't, ever, ever, ever give up. Okay?"

"Okay," Josh answered nodding his head.

"And don't forget to come back and see me when you know what the final stage is," the farmer said as he vanished into the maze.

Chapter 22
Y-Process

On the way home, Dharma got to listen to her two favorite things: country music and Josh's voice as he told her everything he'd learned from the farmer. She was so happy to listen to him that she decided to forgo sticking her head out the window. He told her about the purpose process and the four stages of growth. The farmer had told him about three stages and had said he would have to figure out the final stage for himself. Josh recited the three stages for her.

Stage 1: Preparation
Stage 2: Planting
Stage 3: Growth

To Dharma, it all made sense. But she thought the process needed a different name. It needed to be simpler. She thought it should be called the *Y-process*. Dogs keep things simple, after all.

She knew that every human was here for a greater purpose. They just had to be *willing* to be used for a greater purpose before they could discover this purpose. She figured it was a brilliant weeding-out process. Those willing to be used to make a difference would be given the opportunities and resources to make a difference. Those who would serve in small ways would be developed to serve in big ways. The Y-process made it all possible.

As people search for their *why*, or "Y" (i.e., their purpose and meaning in life), they need to start living their small "y," which is simply a way to make a difference. Humans could do this within a job or outside a job. After all, some people don't have jobs, but everyone can make a difference. The key is that once you start living your small *y* and decide to serve, you progress through the four stages Josh talked about and then you find and live your big Y—that is, your unique purpose that was designed for you before you were born.

The Y-process is simple really. Small *y* leads to big Y for those who are willing to serve, grow and to make a difference. In other words, your desire to serve and make a difference turns your small *y* into your big Y—your ultimate purpose.

Although this concept seems easy to understand, it is much harder to actually go through, as Josh was about to find out.

Chapter 23

Stand Out

Josh had hoped his boss would be happy to see him upon his return to the office, but he was more than happy. He was ecstatic when Josh told him he was coming back to work and was ready for a fresh start. First, his boss clapped his hands and shouted, *"Yes!"* Then he got up from his desk and gave Josh a high five, followed by a bear hug. He thought of Josh as a son as much as an employee, and, while he had been hoping Josh would return to work, he had prepared himself for the worst.

"We missed you around here. It's great to have you back. I thought we might have lost you," he said.

"You didn't lose me. You just got a better me," Josh said before thanking his boss for the time off. "The vacation really helped me gain clarity," he said.

"I'm just glad it did you some good."

"It was more than good. It was life changing," Josh said, nodding his head. "Thank you again. I'm ready to get to work," he added before giving his boss another high five.

Then he walked out the door and went to his desk, as his colleagues watched his every move.

Before he sat down, he took a pot with soil, planted the seed the farmer had given him, and placed it on his desk. His dad had always said that mustard seeds were the smallest of seeds, yet they became the largest of all garden plants, so he put the pot on his desk to remind himself that serving others was about the little things—and that the little things were the big things, and the big things were the little things.

He sat down in silence for a few minutes, gathered his thoughts, and made it his mission to stand out at work. It wasn't enough just to show up to work. With passion and purpose to serve, he would stand out at work. No longer would he be mistaken for a piece of furniture. No longer would he be another brick in the wall. He researched companies that stood out in the marketplace and found simple things that made a big difference. Les Schwab Tires employees, for example, make it a habit to run outside to greet customers when they drive up to one of their tire centers. This lets customers know that they were willing to hustle and do whatever it takes to satisfy them. Chick-fil-A closes on Sundays, and that makes the company stand out. In another example, company policy makes it mandatory for Publix Super Markets employees to take customers who inquire about the location of a product to the correct aisle to show them where it's located. They don't just tell customers the aisle number, they show them to the spot on the shelf. In another case, a hospital actually calls patients after their visits to ask whether they were satisfied with their experience. If companies and organizations could decide to offer superior service, individuals could decide to stand out in their own unique way, too, thought Josh.

He had been a musician and now his work was his stage. He had a note to play, and he was determined to play it to the best of his ability. He would stand out by:

1. Never being too busy to help team members. If they needed help, he would be the first one to assist them.
2. Being the hardest-working person on his team.
3. Writing and singing fun songs of encouragement about his team members to enhance the mood of the office when they faced a deadline.

Before long, it became clear that when he decided to put his unique signature on his work and stand out in his own unique way, people took notice. Some colleagues said that Josh was making them look bad by not only working on his projects but helping colleagues with theirs, and others commended him on his work and effort. Kim, from his department, wanted to know if he had gone to a spa to recharge, because he had come back with so much energy. "I didn't go to a spa," replied Josh. "I just made a choice. I could work for a paycheck or I could make a difference. I decided to make a difference."

He was convinced that people get burned out not because of the work they do, but because they forget why they do it. His restaurant experience and seeing his brother in action had reminded him of his love of serving, and it was his server's heart that changed everything. He wasn't just working for his company. He was working to serve others and to help them become better versions of themselves. He was working for his own learning and growth. And he was working for a power higher than his boss and the CEO. It didn't matter whether some of his superiors or colleagues were negative. It didn't matter if they were having a bad day. It didn't matter if they didn't recognize his work. He decided he was working for an audience of one.

Although the company manual contained a job description for the job performed by Josh, he wrote a new description for himself and put it on his desk. A job and a purpose were two distinct things, he thought, and while you don't need a job to have a purpose, he decided to make his job a vehicle for his purpose. His simple description was "to serve, innovate, and communicate with purpose," and it drove everything he did.

Chapter 24

Growth

A year had gone by, and Josh was as energized and passionate as the day he had come back to work. He looked at the plant in his office and smiled, knowing the seed had become a plant that was growing along with him. Good thing he had an office that could accommodate it. His boss had been promoted, and Josh had been chosen to take his place. Although his new office was larger, he was more comfortable outside of it, rubbing elbows with the rest of his team.

He knew his team cared less about employee parties than they did about having work they loved to do. After all, everyone has a good time at employee parties and gatherings. Everyone is happy when they are playing. It's how you feel while you are working that counts. It's about work being meaningful. It's about work being rewarding. Josh did his best to create a nurturing environment in which all of his team members could plant their own seeds.

As a result of Josh's approach, the leaders in the company began taking notice of his performance and the performance of his team. At leadership meetings, they would put the spotlight on him and talk about the great work he was doing. Josh had come to realize that once you begin to seek out opportunities to make others' lives better, your purpose starts to move through you, and you accomplish amazing things. The key is to have a driving force in your life. For him, it was his faith and his purpose. He didn't talk about it—he lived it.

Ideas about purpose being the driving force for individuals and organizations started to brew in his mind and heart. He researched organizations that were focused on their purpose and found great companies that had a powerful driving force behind them. One of his favorites was an organic dairy company. He spoke to its leaders on the phone and found that they didn't have "sales number goals." Rather, they were extremely focused on their purpose. Of course, they had to forecast numbers, and they measured numbers, but they did so with the belief that numbers were just an indicator or a by-product of how well they were living and sharing their purpose.

Instead of number goals, the company focused on providing opportunities for farmers to make a living. It focused on the sustainability of the land. It focused on providing families with healthy dairy products that were free of hormones and antibiotics. The vice president of marketing told Josh that if they focused on numbers and didn't hit those numbers, then their employees would feel like failures, and morale and engagement would plummet. It's great to focus on numbers when the numbers are always going up, Josh thought. But if the numbers go down and everyone gets depressed, that's not good for business.

He learned that when a company focuses on its purpose instead of numbers, everyone is passionate and energized and this energy fuels performance and enhances the bottom line. Interestingly enough, by focusing on its purpose, the organic dairy company's numbers and profits soared every year. Employees measured numbers, but it just wasn't their main focus. Purpose was their focus, and it drove the numbers way up.

Josh realized that it's not the numbers that drive people, it's your people and purpose that drive the numbers. He wondered whether this would work at his company, and he was getting the feeling that he could do bigger things with these ideas. When he would take action on these ideas, he didn't know. He just had a feeling these ideas were part of his future. As the farmer had told him, ideas, events, and situations would present themselves for his growth. He was in the growth phase. That meant he would experience conditions for growth. However, it meant he would face obstacles, too.

Chapter 25
Tests

Dharma could sense that big things were happening. She could tell because of the way Josh acted and also because he told her about the events of his workday. He told her about his research on the organic milk company, and a few months later, at a leadership meeting, he presented the concept to the leaders of his company. He called it *purpose-driven goals* and suggested that the company should focus on its purpose instead of its numbers. When one of the "energy vampires," as Josh called them, asked him what this purpose would be, he said, "As a company, we will innovate and serve with purpose." He told the leaders that purpose should drive everything they do as a company. He showed them slides, "Sell with Purpose," "Manufacture with Purpose," "Communicate with Purpose." It had been the driving force behind his success, he told them, and it could take the company to a new level.

The CEO loved the concept, whereas several executives balked at the idea. Support was divided, and when the CEO told him to go forward with the messaging and provide a plan for rolling it out to the company, Josh knew that this meant his career would either skyrocket, if it worked, or crash and burn, if it failed. He hadn't realized it before he presented his concept, but he had put himself and his career on the line, and there was nowhere to hide. He didn't have a plan B. All he had was his desire to share his beliefs and faith that his ideas would work.

Over the next few months, Dharma noticed Josh working late all the time on the computer. She would lie down beside him, to let him know he had her full support. He talked to her about everything he was working on and all the challenges he faced. The farmer had said there would be obstacles during the growth phase, and Josh kept reminding himself that setbacks were all part of the process.

"Knowing your purpose is one challenge, but a bigger challenge is finding the courage to follow it and live it in the face of adversity and naysayers," Josh told her.

He also experienced a lot of self-doubt, wondering, "Who am I to be leading such an important initiative?" To make matters worse, his biggest adversaries, two executives from the leadership team, often asked the same question. As Josh and his team rolled out the internal branding campaign to the company, it seemed as though someone at every turn not only questioned his qualifications but also sought to sabotage him and his initiative. The more responsibility he was given, the more others wanted to see him fail. Each success was met with resistance and struggle. Two steps forward was followed by a step backward.

In spite of all the challenges he was facing, Josh had a sense he was on the right path. He felt a greater power pushing him forward and carrying him through the struggles. He was filled with a belief that everything happens for a reason. On the days he wanted to quit and give up, he'd get a call from someone who loved his work, and that person's words of affirmation would fuel him to fight one more day.

Six months after rolling out the campaign to the company, however, Josh's will seemed crushed. When he walked into his apartment, Dharma immediately sensed something was wrong. He wasn't just tired, his spirit was gone. She came over to him and tried to cheer him up, but even dropping the ball on the floor and picking it up didn't make him smile. Josh told her that they had had a leadership meeting, and a review of the numbers revealed that his campaign was not only *not* helping sales—it was actually hurting them. Sales had fallen substantially, and many blamed it on the campaign. Josh told company leaders that this was part of the process as they shifted to a new way of thinking and acting. He asked for more time for the power of purpose to replace the focus on short-term results. But his pleas fell on deaf ears, and he was told they were likely going to pull the plug on the initiative. That night he didn't work on his computer. He didn't listen to music. He went to bed with his clothes on and fell asleep.

Chapter 26

A Dream Remembered

Josh had planned on not going into work the next day. He planned to call in sick. But when he woke up the next morning, he changed his mind. He had the same dream about planting the seed on his desk and then replanting it in a large field where it grew steadily as fruit started to fall off. The dream was starting to make sense. He had planted himself where he was now, and he was growing. He still wasn't sure what the fruit falling off the tree was all about, but the dream reminded him of what the farmer had said about people giving up during the growth phase. The farmer said too many people gave up just as they were about to enter the final stage of purpose. He looked at Dharma and realized he was about to give up too soon. He was about to fail the tests. His purpose and passion needed to be bigger than his challenges. He couldn't give up without standing up for what he believed. With a renewed sense of determination, Josh decided to go to work and put his career and his future on the line. If it didn't work out, he would have to find a new place to replant himself, as George had said. However, if it worked, he knew it would lead to the greatest feeling in the world. Either way, he would grow in the direction of his dreams. He picked up his guitar and played, "Livin' on a Prayer," by Bon Jovi.

An hour later, as Josh walked into the office, he thought about the importance of having dreams, both when you are sleeping and awake. But it's the dreams you have while awake that ignite your soul and inspire you to accomplish things you never thought possible. "My initiative is a dream worth pursuing and worth fighting for," he thought as he sat down in his office and prepared for a meeting with his boss and the CEO.

Chapter 27
Overcome

One definition for *overcome* is "to be helpless." A second definition is "to triumph." When Josh walked into the CEO's office, he felt helpless. When he walked out, he felt triumphant. His passion and conviction were so powerful that the CEO gave his campaign six more months to prove itself. He agreed with Josh that his campaign needed some time to permeate the organization.

In the months that followed, Josh learned firsthand what it took to drive change through an organization. It wasn't just about sharing great ideas. It was about developing relationships with people who would serve as a network for spreading ideas. He should have known, because he grew up in a family that believed everything in life was about relationships, but, as is always the case, experience is the best teacher.

He also developed a love for affecting change in others and saw that by changing people's beliefs and behaviors you could change their lives and careers. Most important, the struggles he faced in trying to make the campaign a success helped him hone his skills as a communicator.

His challenges lead to growth; his delays led to strength; and his belief in the power of communication became another driving force in his life. As the farmer had told him, his purpose was coming into focus. He couldn't articulate it in a sentence, but for the first time in his life Josh had a good idea of why he was here on earth.

Chapter 28
Making A Difference

After six months had gone by, it was clear that Josh had not only overcome his critics at work, but he had overcome the fear, hopelessness, and obstacles that cause people to stop pursuing their purpose and dreams.

His campaign was starting to work, people were buying in, and sales were growing. He also received many e-mails from colleagues thanking him for making a difference in their lives. With a focus on purpose, they not only improved their work lives, they improved their home lives, too. Josh discovered that one person in an organization or family who decides to make a difference enhances the lives of everyone around him or her. The fact that Josh was impacting families of his colleagues was truly rewarding.

Customers and their employees were also buying into the messages. Josh was asked to speak at several clients' events to discuss the importance of purpose-driven goals and the effect purpose can have on the people in an organization. Josh was not only effecting change in the people of his company, he was now impacting people in other companies as well. Josh's career wasn't on the line anymore. Now it was soaring to new heights.

After a celebratory after-work meeting with the leaders of the company, Josh went home to his apartment and Dharma. He looked out the window and felt the pulse of the city. People were still rushing aimlessly from one place to the next, but thankfully, he no longer felt numb and lost like them. He grabbed his guitar and thought about all the people who had encouraged him and helped him arrive at this moment. We all have a seed in us waiting to be planted, he thought. Once planted, our seed needs support, nourishment, and light. *He believed everyone that comes into your life is there for a reason.* Mentors, encouragers, and advice from strangers feed us, provide food for the soul, and give our seed the light it needs to grow and he felt fortunate to have such people guide him along the way. He looked forward to seeing the farmer again after he knew what the final stage was. He then closed his eyes and performed "Stairway to Heaven" for his one and only groupie, Dharma.

Chapter 29

A Name Means Something

I'm glad I don't have a name like other dogs, Dharma thought. Dog names were so predictable: Buddy, Max, Princess, Lady, Caesar, Daisy. Dharma was an uncommon name. Most humans have forgotten that a name means something. Three thousand years ago, when individuals went through a transformative process in life, their name would change. The name change would reflect the transformation they had gone through and their calling in life. The name had a meaning to it. *Joseph*, for example, means "God will increase." *Matthew* means "gift of God." *David* means "beloved." *Kathryn* means "pure." Names are important. A name means something.

Josh had a friend with a baby named Koa. *Koa* means "fearless." I love that name, Dharma thought. She knew her name meant something, too. *Dharma* means "calling," or "your life's purpose." Yes, she knew her life's purpose. It was to love unconditionally and show humans what unconditional love was all about. Josh was her purpose, and she loved him more than anything.

Josh's name meant something, too. The name *Joshua* means "God rescues." It wasn't surprising, then, that as Josh matured and went through a transformation process over a few years, Dharma noticed he now preferred to be called *Joshua* instead of *Josh*. It made perfect sense. He was entering into a new phase in his life. He was becoming all he was supposed to be. His calling was clear. There's nothing more exciting than a dog or human who represents the meaning of the name they were given. Yes, a name means something.

Chapter 30
Abundance

Joshua stood onstage, guitar in hand, microphone in front of him, looking out at the crowd. A few thousand people were waiting for him to speak. He couldn't believe it had been five years since his boss gave him an ultimatum, the farmer gave him a seed, the pilot gave him perspective, Solomon gave him hope, the past gave him a gift, and George gave him a sign.

After the success of the *purpose* campaign, his work and life had changed dramatically. He had gone from being an employee at his company to being a thought leader in the industry. His CEO had asked Joshua to write a blog sharing his philosophies. It was an independent blog, separate from the company, yet one that positioned the company as a forerunner in the marketplace.

Joshua called his blog "The Seed," and it included all his musings about growing a life, a business, and a career with purpose. And, like the seed, the blog's popularity grew enormously, as did Joshua's profile and exposure. He became a featured speaker at numerous conferences on branding, communication, and marketing, which is why he found himself onstage on this day.

He asked the audience how they were doing, and the crowd responded, "Great!" He gave a big smile to the crowd, knowing that five years ago he hadn't just planted a seed on his desk—he had also planted a seed in his heart. And this seed grew into a purpose that grew into a mission that grew into a dream that he was now living.

He started playing the guitar and sang a short melody: *"Dreams can come true. Dreams can happen to you. If you let your purpose live through you."* The crowd cheered.

Joshua looked up and smiled. He wasn't meant to be a minister. He wasn't meant to be a musician. He was meant to do what he was doing right now. Everything in his past had prepared him for this moment and the purpose he was living and sharing. He was playing his note and contributing to the one song. He put his guitar down, grabbed the microphone, and passionately said, "If you want to truly be successful, your desire to make a difference has to be greater than your desire to make money. If it is, then you will accomplish both."

Once again, the audience cheered, and Joshua was reminded of what his purpose was. It had become so clear he could share it in an elevator with a stranger: *"to positively change people's hearts, minds, and actions through the power of communication and purpose."* He had been given the gift to communicate through speech, music, writing, marketing, and branding, and he would use all these vehicles to influence others in a positive way. He discovered that, for organizations to change, people had to change. And for people to change, their beliefs had to change. Changed beliefs would lead to changed behaviors, which would lead to changed habits and new outcomes. He wanted to change the world, but he knew that changing the world happened one person at a time. And the driving force behind this change was the power of purpose.

Each person has unique gifts and a unique purpose, and Joshua used the power of communication to help people search for it, find it, live it, and share it. He told every audience and every person he met what he had discovered in his own life. When you plant yourself where you are and decide to make a difference, instead of searching for your purpose, it finds you.

He told the audience, "We think we'll get excited about life when we get a life that is exciting. But just the opposite is true. When we get excited about life, we get a life that is exciting.

"Passion and purpose are like neighbors who are best friends. They always hang out together. Deciding to be passionate about life and work leads you to your purpose. And when you're purposeful, you unleash your passion. Every cell in your body lights up when you are living and working with passion and purpose."

Joshua's favorite part of his talk was sharing stories of people who had found their purpose and shared it. He talked about the salesperson who was number one in her company because her goal was to make more money so she could give more to charity. He spoke of the entrepreneur who built a business as a vehicle for his passion and purpose and is not only making a fortune but changing countless lives. He shared the story of the loan officer of a mortgage company who told him that her job was to save people's marriages, because in helping people keep their homes she would be helping to keep families together. Not surprisingly, she thrived in her industry. He talked about a dental practice that made "smiling faces" its purpose—and about a professional football player who said his purpose was to glorify God on the football field.

Everywhere he went, people shared their stories with him. He met people from all walks of life—accountants, artists, medical professionals, architects, construction workers, athletes, educators, stay-at-home moms, and the like—who shared how they were able to use their unique gifts for a greater purpose. Joshua was amazed at the mosaic of talents that existed on the planet and how these collection of talents formed society as a whole. "Just imagine," he said to the audience, "if everyone had the same gifts and talents. Imagine if everyone had the same purpose. We wouldn't be able to function as a society. You were born with a purpose, not just for you, but also for a bigger purpose beyond you. You were made to contribute to others and to the world, and each one of us is the beneficiary of the talents and purpose of our neighbors, colleagues, and fellow human beings. To not seek your purpose and to not live it is to deny the gifts you are meant to share with others."

Joshua wasn't just impacting his company. He was now reaching people in organizations around the world. He received many wonderful e-mails and stories describing how his principles and concepts were influencing other people and their work. His influence had grown so much that the CEO of his company made him an offer.

After his speech, he went home and told Dharma all about it over dinner. While she ate he talked. The CEO had given him a choice: He could become the president of his company, or he could start his own consulting company and his former company would be his first client. The leaders in his company knew he was outgrowing his role there, and they didn't want to lose him: They would be happy to work with him in either scenario.

Both offers included a lot of money, but Joshua didn't care about money. Abundance in the form of money, happiness, and friendships was a by-product of playing your note and contributing to the symphony of life.

He rubbed Dharma's back, then walked to the window and looked at the plant growing outside. The plant had become too big for his office, so he had planted it in the garden outside his apartment, where a larger field would allow it to spread its roots and continue to grow.

"I think I know what the final stage of purpose is," he said cheerfully to Dharma. He thought of the farmer and remembered the farmer asking him to come back after he had figured out what the final stage was. Joshua looked in the mirror. He had changed a lot in the past five years. He once was lost but now was found, and he decided to go back to the place where his journey first started. It was the Thanksgiving holiday, and he had a week off to recharge, visit his family, and think about the direction of his future. He would visit the farm and then drive to his parents' home, as he had five years ago, but this time under much difference circumstances.

Chapter 31

A Season for Everything

The seasons teach us that there is a time and a purpose for everything. There is a time to prepare, a time to plant, a time to grow, and a time to harvest.

Joshua arrived at the farm as the land was preparing to rest for the winter in order to recharge itself for another season of planting and growing. Joshua knew about the purpose of seasons. He had experienced them in his own growth process. He had gone through the preparation stage, the planting stage, the growth stage, and was now experiencing the greatest feeling in the world associated with the final stage.

He walked around the farm as Dharma waited in the car. It was a cold, sunny day, and the farm, like the land, was quiet and still. The once mighty and scary corn maze had fallen victim to the cycle of life, and all that remained were lifeless cornstalks on the ground.

Joshua walked toward the farmhouse, hoping the farmer would be around. It had been five years since he had been here, and he knew that the farmer might be anywhere but here. But it was worth a shot to try to see him. He had changed his life, and in this season of gratitude he wanted to say thank you.

The farmhouse was empty except for a few pieces of furniture, some corn maze T-shirts, souvenirs, and a few pictures on the wall. Joshua walked over to one of the pictures and noticed it was the farmer he had met in the maze. As he looked at the picture, an elderly woman came out of the kitchen and dining area where Joshua had eaten lunch with his friends five years ago.

"That's my Paul," she said. Joshua felt embarrassed that he had not known the farmer's name. He should have asked.

"Where is he?" Joshua inquired. "I've been thinking a lot about him and was hoping to speak to him."

The woman smiled. "I'd love to speak to him, too. In fact, I often do. He just doesn't speak back."

"Is he sick?" Joshua asked, now more concerned about the farmer's health than about telling him that he knew what the final stage was.

The woman paused, as tears welled up in her eyes. "My Paul is gone," she said. "He passed away. He was such a wonderful man, and I miss him dearly. He was my best friend."

"I'm so sorry," Joshua said, as he placed his hand over his heart. He didn't know what else to say, and he stood looking at the picture in awkward silence, remembering the farmer's youthful radiance and sparkling blue eyes.

"I came back to see him," Joshua said sadly. "I wanted to thank him for making a difference in my life. When I saw him five years ago I was as lost as they come. Now I know what I'm here on earth for."

The woman's tears turned into a smile. It wasn't the first time she had heard such kind words about her husband. She turned to Joshua, grabbed his face with her frail, cold hands, and said, "Young man, my husband has been gone for 10 years."

"What do you mean? Are you sure? I saw him in the maze five years ago. I saw him twice within a few weeks," Joshua said, searching his brain for possible explanations. Perhaps in her old age the woman had lost her sense of time, he thought.

"I'm sure," said the woman, sharing the date and year of his death.

Joshua shook his head. He knew things happened that defied explanation, but they were always stories about someone else. Not him.

More tears streamed from her eyes as she thought about the difference her husband had made in people's lives.

"Yes, another harvest," she said to herself. "The love continues to grow." It wasn't the first time she had experienced a person coming to the farm to thank her Paul. She had met hundreds of people who said they met her husband in the maze. And each time it made her cry. Not because she was sad, but because she was filled with joy.

"You know, you're not the first person tell me this," she said reassuringly to Joshua. "You're not crazy, I promise. Hundreds of people have met my husband in the maze. His body may be gone, but he's still here planting seeds. At first I thought these people were crazy, but there have been too many of them to think they were all hallucinating. Then I realized that maybe I'm the crazy one for not believing.

"When Paul was alive, he loved two things: planting seeds and talking about purpose. He would talk about purpose all the time. He was fascinated with it. He would write down ideas about the stages of purpose, which didn't make much sense to me, but obviously there's a bunch of people who understand what he was talking about. He often said that his purpose is to help others live theirs. He loved helping people who were lost. They all come back saying he made a difference in their life. He's just doing now what he always loved to do. He's planting a love that grows, and you are his harvest, young man," the woman said, placing her hand on Joshua's shoulder.

"My name is Joshua," he said as he hugged the old woman. "I appreciate you taking the time to tell me this. I'm sorry for your loss, but I'm thankful your husband is not done planting seeds." He then walked with her to the door and outside to the porch of the farmhouse. From there he could see the remnants of the maze where he had met the farmer. Was it a real? A vision? An illusion? It didn't matter. The seed planted in his heart was real. The change in his life was real. The difference he was making was real. He wanted to tell the farmer what the final stage was. But he had a feeling the farmer already knew that he had discovered it. He said good-bye to the farmer's wife and walked slowly to his car, taking in the fresh air and the sights of the farm one last time. The farm might be preparing for rest, but Joshua was ready for a harvest.

Chapter 32

The Harvest

Joshua told Dharma about the final stage as they drove away from the farm. He had gone through the preparation stage, the planting stage, the growth stage, and was now in the fourth and final stage, the *harvest stage*, in which all your preparation, hard work, growth, and faith throughout the tests pay off. "This is the stage where you reap the harvest you have sown with your seed.

"During the harvest stage, your purpose becomes so clear you can say it in a simple sentence," Joshua told her. It's a time of great abundance. During the harvest, there is nothing you lack. You give, you give, and you give, and you are replenished. What you give comes back to you exponentially. You produce much fruit in the form of benefits to others and to the world, and in turn this fruit becomes a seed for others to plant.

"When you reach the harvest stage, you are able to look back and see how all the stages are connected. Your past prepares you to be planted. You plant yourself so you can grow. You grow so you can produce a harvest that will produce fruit. And your fruit produces seeds in others that change lives. The duration of the stages may be different for each person, but the cycle is the same. The cycle has a purpose. You plant yourself so that you can reap a harvest that will help others become all they are meant to be. The cycle then begins in others who are willing to plant themselves where they are so they in turn can produce a harvest for others. Joshua was the farmer's harvest, and the people he impacted would be his harvest.

His dream now made perfect sense. He was living the system designed for his growth and the growth of others. The dream was telling him that as long as you have a seed in your hand and heart, you have the power to create a harvest. Yet for the harvest to happen, you must sow your seed. You must plant yourself, because unless the seed dies and goes into the ground it can't bring forth fruit. You must do the work, and when you do, your small purpose will grow into your bigger purpose and you will be given a bigger field to grow to produce a bigger harvest.

He looked at his past and saw a vision for his future and knew that his preparation, planting, growth and the harvest he produced weren't just for his benefit. The harvest he produced was for all the people who would benefit from the fruit of his gifts, talents, work, and life.

Joshua thought of the two job offers from his CEO. He still wasn't sure which offer he would take. Both opportunities would allow him to make a difference in the lives of others. Both jobs would provide a bigger field for him to continue to grow and produce more fruit. Both jobs would allow him to live and share his bigger purpose. He wasn't going to rush into a decision. He would patiently wait and look for the signs that would help him make the right decision. There was a path set for him, and he knew he just had to follow the signs and make the decisions that kept him on the path.

As he drove along the open highway, he looked up for a brief second and promised that whichever job he took, he would continue planting his seed: to grow himself to be a bigger benefit to others, to produce a bigger harvest for the world, and to plant more seeds in others. Just because he was in the harvest stage didn't mean he was finished growing. More growth would mean more fruit and more seeds to plant. Like Paul, he would be a seed giver. He would hand seeds to people and encourage them to find their purpose. Joshua turned up the radio to listen to one of Dharma's favorite songs, and she barked her approval. He turned to Dharma. "So, what do you think, girl? Which job offer should I take?" Dharma perked up. She knew the answer and wanted to tell him but couldn't. After all, there are things in life that humans have to figure out for themselves.

The End!

Life is about you. If it weren't about you, you wouldn't be here.
>   You are not an accident.
>   You are here for a reason.
>   You have a destiny.
>   You have a purpose.
>   You have gifts and talents.
>   You do things that only you can do in the way you do them.
>   You and only you can leave your mark on the world.

Life is about more than you. It's about knowing you were made for relationships:
>   To love
>   To mentor
>   To learn
>   To serve
>   To create
>   To work together
>   To change for the better

It's about living for more than you.
>   For a bigger purpose.
>   For a greater cause.
>   For those who will become your legacy.

It's about you knowing you are part of something much bigger than you.
>   You live in a universe.
>   *Uni-verse* means "one song."
>   Songs don't happen by accident.
>   Songs are created by organizing notes into arrangements and patterns.
>   And so there is a Creator of the one song.
>   You are an expression of the Creator.
>   You are a note in the greatest of symphonies.

It's about you!
>   It's about you contributing to the one song.
>   It's about you playing your part to the best of your ability.
>   It's about you lifting others up.
>   It's about you living the purpose God created you for.
>   It's about you, the Creator, and the song becoming one.

Life is about you, and *what you do* is up to you.

Other Books by Jon Gordon

The Energy Bus

A man whose life and career are in shambles learns from a unique bus driver and set of passengers how to overcome adversity. Enjoy an enlightening ride of positive energy that is improving the way leaders lead, employees work, and teams function.

www.TheEnergyBus.com

The No Complaining Rule

Follow a VP of Human Resources who must save herself and her company from ruin, and discover proven principles and an actionable plan to win the battle against individual and organizational negativity.

www.NoComplainingRule.com

Training Camp

This inspirational story about a small guy with a big heart, and a special coach who guides him on a quest for excellence, reveals the eleven winning habits that separate the best individuals and teams from the rest.

www.TrainingCamp11.com

The Shark and the Goldfish

Delightfully illustrated, this quick read is packed with tips and strategies on how to respond to challenges beyond your control in order to thrive during waves of change.

www.SharkandGoldfish.com

Soup

The newly appointed CEO of a popular soup company is brought in to reinvigorate the brand and bring success back to a company that has fallen on hard times. Through her journey, discover the key ingredients to unite, engage, and inspire teams to create a culture of greatness.

www.Soup11.com

One Word

One Word is a simple concept that delivers powerful life change! This quick read will inspire you to simplify your life and work by focusing on just one word for this year. *One Word* creates clarity, power, passion, and life-change. When you find your word, live it, and share it, your life will become more rewarding and exciting than ever.

www.getoneword.com

The Positive Dog

We all have two dogs inside of us. One dog is positive, happy, optimistic, and hopeful. The other dog is negative, mad, pessimistic, and fearful. These two dogs often fight inside us, but guess who wins? The one you feed the most. *The Positive Dog* is an inspiring story that not only reveals the strategies and benefits of being positive, but also an essential truth: being positive doesn't just make you better; it makes everyone around you better.

www.feedthepositivedog.com

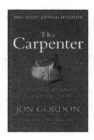

The Carpenter

The Carpenter is Jon Gordon's most inspiring book yet—filled with powerful lessons and success strategies. Michael wakes up in the hospital with a bandage on his head and fear in his heart after collapsing during a morning jog. When Michael finds out the man who saved his life is a carpenter, he visits him and quickly learns that he is more than just a carpenter; he is also a builder of lives, careers, people, and teams. In this journey, you will learn timeless principles to help you stand out, excel, and make an impact on people and the world.

www.carpenter11.com

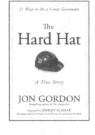

The Hard Hat

A true story about Cornell lacrosse player George Boiardi, *The Hard Hat* is an unforgettable book about a selfless, loyal, joyful, hard-working, competitive, and compassionate leader and teammate, the impact he had on his team and program, and the lessons we can learn from him. This inspirational story will teach you how to build a great team and be the best teammate you can be.

www.hardhat21.com

You Win in the Locker Room First

Based on the extraordinary experiences of NFL Coach Mike Smith and leadership expert Jon Gordon, *You Win in the Locker Room First* offers a rare, behind-the-scenes look at one of the most pressure-packed leadership jobs on the planet, and what leaders can learn from these experiences in order to build their own winning teams.

www.wininthelockerroom.com

Other Books by Jon Gordon

Life Word

Life Word reveals a simple, powerful tool to help you identify the word that will inspire you to live your best life while leaving your greatest legacy. In the process, you'll discover your *why*, which will help show you how to live with a renewed sense of power, purpose, and passion.

www.getoneword.com/lifeword

The Power of Positive Leadership

The Power of Positive Leadership is your personal coach for becoming the leader your people deserve. Jon Gordon gathers insights from his bestselling fables to bring you the definitive guide to positive leadership. Difficult times call for leaders who are up for the challenge. Results are the byproduct of your culture, teamwork, vision, talent, innovation, execution, and commitment. This book shows you how to bring it all together to become a powerfully positive leader.

www.powerofpositiveleadership.com

The Energy Bus Field Guide

The Energy Bus Field Guide is your roadmap to fueling your life, work, and team with positive energy. The international bestseller, *The Energy Bus*, has helped millions of people from around the world shift to a more positive outlook. This guide is a practical companion to help you *live and share* the ten principles from *The Energy Bus* every day, with real, actionable steps you can immediately put into practice in your life, work, team, and organization.

The Power of a Positive Team

In *The Power of a Positive Team*, Jon Gordon draws upon his unique team building experience, as well as conversations with some of the greatest teams in history, to provide an essential framework of proven practices to empower teams to work together more effectively and achieve superior results.

www.PowerOfAPositiveTeam.com

The Coffee Bean

From bestselling author Jon Gordon and rising star Damon West comes *The Coffee Bean*: an illustrated fable that teaches readers how to transform their environment, overcome challenges, and create positive change.

The Energy Bus for Kids

The illustrated children's adaptation of the bestselling book, *The Energy Bus*, tells the story of George, who, with the help of his school bus driver, Joy, learns that if he believes in himself, he'll find the strength to overcome any challenge. His journey teaches kids how to overcome negativity, bullies, and everyday challenges to be their best.

www.EnergyBusKids.com

Thank You and Good Night

Thank You and Good Night is a beautifully illustrated book that shares the heart of gratitude. Jon Gordon takes a little boy and girl on a fun-filled journey from one perfect moonlit night to the next. During their adventurous days and nights, the

Other Books by Jon Gordon

children explore the people, places, and things they are thankful for.

The Hard Hat for Kids

The Hard Hat for Kids is an illustrated guide to teamwork. Adapted from the bestseller *The Hard Hat*, this uplifting story presents practical insights and life-changing lessons that are immediately applicable to everyday situations, giving kids—and adults—a new outlook on cooperation, friendship, and the selfless nature of true teamwork.

www.HardHatforKids.com

The Y-Process

A powerful way to discover and live your purpose

To learn more about our Y-Process workshops visit:

www.Seed11.com

To help your team grow to their full potential contact The Jon Gordon Companies, Inc.:

Phone: (904) 285-6842
E-mail: info@jongordon.com
Online: www.JonGordon.com
Twitter: @JonGordon11
830-13 A1A N.
Suite 111
Ponte Vedra Beach, FL 32082

Sign up for Jon Gordon's weekly e-newsletter at:

www.JonGordon.com

To purchase bulk copies of *The Seed* at a discount for large groups or your organization, please contact your favorite bookseller or Wiley Special Sales at specialsales@wiley.com or (800) 762-2974.